FORD, REGAINING THEIR COMPETITIVE EDGE

Ford, Regaining Their Competitive Edge

A Study of the Strategic Management Processes for Operational Success

Dr. Carl G. Smith Sr.

iUniverse, Inc.

New York Lincoln Shanghai

Ford, Regaining Their Competitive Edge

A Study of the Strategic Management Processes for Operational Success

iUniverse books may be ordered through booksellers or by contacting:

iUniverse
2021 Pine Lake Road, Suite 100
Lincoln, NE 68512
www.iuniverse.com
1-800-Authors (1-800-288-4677)

Because of the dynamic nature of the Internet, any Web addresses or links contained in this book may have changed since publication and may no longer be valid.

The views expressed in this work are solely those of the author and do not necessarily reflect the views of the publisher, and the publisher hereby disclaims any responsibility for them.

ISBN: 978-0-595-47010-5 (pbk)
ISBN: 978-0-595-91295-7 (ebk)

Printed in the United States of America

CONTENTS

Acknowledgements vii

Executive Summary..ix

Abstract...xi

Chapter 1:   Company Introduction.. 1

   Business Description...*1*

   History...*3*

   Ford Motor Company...*4*

   Company and Eli Lilly..*4*

   Homer A Neal...*5*

   Donat R. Leclair *5*

   Major Products and Services...*5*

   Products And Services Analysis *5*

Chapter 2:   Literature Review... 7

   Competitiveness of U.S. Cars in Taiwan..*11*

   A Case Study Background *12*

   The Attribute Selection *12*

   Estimated Fuzzy Weight *12*

   Consumer Purchasing Behavior Analysis *13*

   Swat Analysis *19*

   Strengths Weaknesses..*19*

   Strengths *20*

   Weaknesses *21*

Chapter 3:   Methodology 23

   Research method *27*

Results *31*

Increasing importance of key performance criteria *31*

Outsourcing is increasing *33*

Analysis and findings in relation to existing research *37*

Questionnaire survey results *40*

Chapter 4:   Discussion **48**

Supply chain management system Finding the Best Fit *48*

Ford and information technology *49*

Issues *50*

Further discussion of the present findings *52*

Ford Motor Company's Information Systems *54*

Technology Factors *55*

Organizational Factors *55*

Planning and Standards Development *56*

Discussion's Conclusion The HRD Role *57*

Ford's Most Famous Failure *58*

Chapter 5:   Recommendations **61**

Improvement Tactics Employed by Organizations *61*

Improvement Strategies Employed by Organizations *64*

Quantified Improvements Achieved *70*

Conclusions and suggestions for further research *70*

Appendix **73**

References **85**

Bibliography **89**

Acknowledgements

Grateful acknowledgement is made to a number of people for their, support and guidance throughout the generation of research and the creation of this work. Firstly, personnel at the Warren National University and the Long Island University for their wealth of knowledge, instruction and invaluable guidance.

The author wishes to acknowledge the considerable time and effort of the industry respondents involved in this study.

Finally, the author would like to thank Christopher, Spencer, Aaron, Carl jr., Steven wife Angela and the author's family for their help and support throughout the research.

Executive Summary

This project contains a look into the manufacturing company of Ford Motor Company. Research was done about how the company runs business, both globally and domestically. In this report, the company's mission, goals, strategies, product and service portfolios, market share and profit performance, technology and employment information are outlined. Key successes and weakness failures are also discussed in detail.

Information about Ford's use of computer systems and an information model for the company is also included. The information model displays Ford's Work System, showing which components of the Work Organization, Control System, Industrial Relations and Human Resources Practices Ford implements. The Business Organization, with Ford's Business Strategy and Enterprise Organization is also part of the model. At the end of the report, self-evaluations by team members and references can be found. Ford Motor Company is currently trying to increase its global market share in automobile sales while facing slumping market share numbers in the United States. This report examines the Ford company characteristics and how the company uses information systems in the business climate. Ford believes that having solid relationships with their employees, dealers, suppliers, and stakeholders allows them to have an advantage over their competitors. Healthy professional relationships are helpful to a company's success but being able to attract customers to your products will increase sales.

Ford has recently introduced new vehicle architecture to try and attract new buyers. The largest innovation for Ford has been the introduction of their Hybrid cars. Ford reported an October 2006 sales drop of 23.5 percent as compared to a year ago. The new measures Ford is taking with their automobile design are expected to help those numbers reverse in the future.

Ford sales have also under performed in the global markets although the company is taking steps to increase sales while reducing costs. Ford has recently entered new markets, most of which are located in the Asian-Pacific region. To reduce costs and increase knowledge of a region Ford uses small ERP systems that are less expensive and faster to implement than the larger ERP systems. Failure to obtain a larger market share in foreign markets has hurt the company. Ford got a late start entering the automobile market in China, compared to competitors, and now controls less than one percent of the market share. To add to the situation the Chinese government has high taxes on automobiles that can increase the price up to 100 percent or more. The future of Ford is headed towards a reported implementation of SAP throughout its North America organization. The proper use of information systems by Ford will increase their ability to maintain a successful business in future years locally and globally.

Abstract

Strong competition and structural changes characterize the car manufacturing. A number of trends (i.e. general changes over time) concerning sourcing strategies and supplier relations can therefore be recognized. The article aims to analyze how these trends correspond to the actual situation in the car industry and how Ford Motor Company can get an edge (further). The paper discusses a brilliant study of the strategic implications of the Ford Motor Company, and how the Company can regain its competitive edge.

CHAPTER 1

▼

COMPANY INTRODUCTION

Ford Motor Company (Ford) is one of the largest automotive manufacturers in the world. Ford motors, manufacture and distribute automobiles in 200 markets across six continents. The company's automotive vehicle brands include Aston Martin, Ford, Jaguar, Land Rover, Lincoln, Mazda, Mercury and Volvo. The company primarily operates in the US and Europe. It is headquartered in Dearborn, Michigan and employs about 300,000 people.

The organization recorded revenues of $177,089 million during the fiscal year ended December 2005, an increase of 3.2% in excess of 2004. The operating income of the company was $7,493 million during fiscal year 2005, a decrease of 37% from 2004. The net profit was $2,024 million in fiscal year 2005, a reduction of 42% from 2004.

Business Description

Ford is one of the Big Three manufacturers in the US. The other companies in the Big Three include DaimlerChrysler and General Motors. The company manufactures and distributes automobiles in 200 markets across six continents. With 108 plants worldwide, the company's core and affiliated automotive brands include Aston Martin, Ford, Jaguar, Land Rover, Lincoln, Mazda, Mercury and Volvo. It also owns a 33.4% controlling stake in Mazda.

The company operates in two businesses: automotive and financial services. The automotive business consists of the design, development, manufacture, sale and service of cars, trucks and service parts. Through this segment, Ford produces a wide range of vehicles including cars for the small, medium, large and premium segments, trucks, buses/vans (including minivans), full-size pickups, sport utility vehicles and vehicles for the medium/heavy segments. The company's automotive business is organized into two primary segments: Americas; Ford Europe Premier Automotive Group; and Ford Asia Pacific and Africa/Mazda.

The American segment primarily includes the sale of Ford, Lincoln and Mercury brand vehicles and related service parts in North America (the US, Canada and Mexico) and Ford-brand vehicles and related service parts in South America. The Ford Europe and Premier Automotive Group primarily includes the sale of Fordbrand vehicles and related service parts in Europe and Turkey and the sale of Premier Automotive Group (PAG) brand vehicles (Volvo, Jaguar, Land Rover and Aston Martin) and related service parts throughout the world (including North and South America, Asia Pacific and Africa).

Ford Asia Pacific and Africa/Mazda segment primarily includes the sale of Ford-brand vehicles and related service parts in the Asia Pacific region and South Africa, and Ford's share of the results of Mazda Motor Corporation and certain of other Mazda related investments. In addition to producing and selling cars and trucks, Ford also provides retail customers with a range of after sales services and products through its dealer network. The company provides services such as maintenance and light repair, heavy repair, collision, vehicle accessories and extended service warranty. In North America, the company markets these products and services under several brands, including Genuine Ford and Lincoln-Mercury Parts and Service, Ford Extended Service Plan (ESP) and Motor craft.

The financial services segment operates through the company subsidiary, Ford Motor Credit Company (Ford Credit). Ford Credit offers a wide variety of automotive financing products to, and through automotive dealers throughout the world. The predominant share of Ford Credit's business consists of financing Ford vehicles and supporting the company's dealers. Ford Credit's primary financial products fall into the three categories retail financing, wholesale financing and other financing. In retail financing Ford engages in purchasing retail installment sales contracts and retail lease contracts from dealers. The company also offers financing to commercial customers comprising vehicle leasing companies and fleet purchasers. In wholesale financing, Ford offers loans to dealers to finance the purchase of vehicle inventory. In other financing, Ford makes loans to dealers for working capital, improvements to dealership facilities, and for acquiring and refinancing real estate. Ford Credit also services the finance receivables and leases that it originates and purchases, makes loans to affiliates, purchases receivables from company subsidiaries, and provides selected insurance services.

History

Ford was established in 1903 by Henry Ford and 11 other associates. The company made its first shipment in the same year. The company launched its T model in 1908. The company began producing trucks and tractors in 1917. During 1925, Ford acquired the Lincoln Motor Company, branching out into luxury cars. In 1956, Ford went public. In the same decade, Ford produced one of its most successful cars: the Thunderbird. The global expansion of Ford continued during the 1960s when the company established Ford Europe in 1967. Throughout the 1970s and 1980s, Ford continued to expand, with further moves into Europe and Asia. In 1987, Ford helped to form the Park Ridge Corporation in order to acquire the Hertz car rental business. Ford experienced further growth in the 2005s. In 1990, Ford acquired Jaguar. The company increased its stake in Hertz to 100% in 2005. The company acquired the repair chain Kiwi-Fit in 2004 and later Volvo's passenger vehicle business. Ford spun off its Visteon automotive components business unit during 2000. Ford also acquired Land Rover from BMW in the same year. In late 2002, the company concluded the sale of Collision Team of America (CTA) and Kiwi-Fit. Ford expanded its presence in China during 2002 and 2003. The Changan Ford (a joint venture operation with Changan Automobile) assembly plant located in Chongqing became operational and production of the Fiesta in China started in mid 2003. The company's Ford Services Thailand became operational later in 2003.

Ford sold Cosworth, its motor sport technology engineering company, and Jaguar Racing, its Formula One team, during 2004. Also in 2004, the company recalled about 600,000 vehicles of its Escape and Mazda Tribute SUVs. In the same year, the company launched the 2005 F-Series Super Duty and has also introduced the Ford Expedition King Ranch. Ford recalled about 792,000 pickup trucks and sport utility vehicles, during January 2005, because of a fire risk from overheating of the speed control switch. The recall involves some of Ford's 2000 model-year F-150 pickup trucks, Expedition and Navigator SUVs, and 2001 model-year F-Series Super crew pickup trucks

Edge

4   Ford, Regaining Their Competitive Edge

equipped with speed control. The company made several acquisitions during 2005. This included the reacquisition of Visitor's twenty-three North American facilities in order to protect its supply of components. The company also acquired a minority interest in the Beanstalk Group, a majority-owned subsidiary that licensed trademarks, and subsequently sold 100% interest in the Beanstalk Group.

Ford sold its subsidiary The Hertz Corporation, one of the largest general use car rental businesses in the world, during 2005. Ford also sold its interests in Marinara & Marinara and Vastera during the same year. The company also exchanged its 8.3 million shares in Ballard Power Systems for an equity interest in NuCellSys, a 50:50 joint venture with DaimlerChrysler In July 2006, Ford became the first automotive manufacturer to commence the production of dedicated hydrogen fueled V-10 engines.

Ford Motor Company

Key Employee Biographies Ms. Marram is a Non Executive Director of Ford. She served as Managing Director of North Castle Partners during 2000. Ms. Marram served as President and Chief Executive Officer of Efdex from 2004 to 2000. She previously served as President and Chief Executive Officer of Tropicana Beverage Group from 2004 until 2004, and had previously served as President of the group, as well as Executive Vice President of The Seagram Company and Joseph E. Seagram & Sons. Before joining Seagram in 2005, she served as President and Chief Executive Officer of Nabisco Biscuit Company and Senior Vice President of the Nabisco Foods Group from 1988 until 2005. She has also been a Director of The New York Times

Company and Eli Lilly

Board: Non Executive Board Job Title: Director Since: 2005 Mr. Thornton is a Non Executive Director of Ford. He retired as President and Co Chief Operating Officer of The Goldman Sachs Group in 2003. Mr. Thornton has served as Chairman of Goldman Sachs, Asia from 2005 to 2004. He was previously Co-Chief Executive of Goldman Sachs International, the firm's business in Europe, the Middle East and Africa. He joined Goldman Sachs in 1980 and was appointed a Partner in 1988.

Homer A Neal

Board: Non Executive Board Job Title: Director Since: 2004 Dr. Neal is a Non Executive Director of Ford. He is Director, University of Michigan Atlas Project, Samuel A. Goudsmit distinguished professor of Physics and interim president emeritus at the University of Michigan. Dr. Neal joined the University as Chairman of its Physics Department in 1987 and in 2005 was appointed Vice President of Research. Dr. Neal served as Interim President of the University of Michigan from 2005 to 2004. He has served as a Member of the US National Science Board and of the Advisory Board of the Oak Ridge National Laboratory.

Donat R. Leclair

Board: Senior Management Job Title: Executive Vice President Mr. Leclair is a Non Executive Director of Ford. Mr. Leclair served as the company's Controller during 2001. Previously, he served as Controller for North America. He joined Ford in 1976 as a Financial Analyst at the Lorain Assembly Plant and has held various leadership positions in product development, manufacturing and finance.

Major Products and Services

Ford Motor Company is one of the largest automotive manufacturers in the world. It manufactures and distributes automobiles in 200 markets across six continents. The company's key products and services include the following:

Products: Passenger cars trucks buses and vans sport utility vehicles vehicle accessories, after sales vehicle parts and products extended repair service products services: maintenance and vehicle repair services financial services:

Retail financing Wholesale financing Third-party claim management services Brands:

Ford Mercury Lincoln Volvo Jaguar Land Rover Aston Martin

Products And Services Analysis

The company recorded revenues of $177,089 million during the fiscal year ended December 2005, an increase of 3.2% over 2004. For the fiscal year 2005, the Americas, the company's largest geographic market, accounted for 55.4% of the total revenues.

Ford generates revenues through two business divisions: automotive (86.7% of the total revenues during fiscal year 2005) and financial services (13.3%). Revenues by Division During the fiscal year 2005, the automotive division recorded revenues of $153,503 million, an increase of 4.3% over 2004. The financial services division recorded revenues of $23,586 million in fiscal year 2005, a decrease of 3.8% from 2004. Revenues by Geography the Americas, Ford's largest geographical market, accounted for 55.4% of the total revenues in the fiscal year 2005. Revenues from The Americas reached $85,000 million in 2005, a decrease of 1.2% from 2004. Ford Europe and PAG accounted for 39.3% of the total revenues in the fiscal year 2005. Revenues from Ford Europe and PAG reached $60,258 million in 2005, an increase of 11.3% over 2004.

Ford Asia, Africa and Ford Mazda accounted for 5.3% of the total revenues in the fiscal year 2005. Revenues from Ford Asia, Africa and Ford Mazda reached $8,245 million in 2005, an increase of 18.5% over 2004.

CHAPTER 2

▼

LITERATURE REVIEW

Consumers make many purchase decisions in their lives. Some decisions are rather simple and easy to make, whereas others are complex and difficult. In order to simplify the consumer's decision-making processes, marketers find ways to create better products and improve marketing mixes.

Recently, marketers have become interested in the specific decision rules that consumers use when selecting a product. These rules may involve the attributes actually considered when making a purchase (Runyon & Stewart, 1987). For example, consumers might use such attributes as price, length of warranty, miles per gallon, and so on, in making judgments about which automobile they prefer and want to purchase. Like many durable goods purchases, the automobile consumer's purchasing behavior involves making multiple-attribute decisions. In general the Multiple-Attribute Utility Model (MAUM) is the preferred model in the application of multiple decision-making in a consumer purchasing behavior study. Because MAUM also uses utility theory, it can show consumers' attitudes towards multiple attributes of a product. However, consumer preference of product attributes is a subjective cognition. The values which indicate the preference often contain fuzziness and imprecision. Although it is common to apply MAUM to consumer decision-making, the fuzziness and imprecision of the attributes have never been taken into consideration.

Although Rosenberg was the first (Loudon & Della Bitta, 1979; Jaccard, Brinbery & Lee, 1986) to apply MAUM to a consumer purchasing behavior study, Fishbein presented the well-known Fishbein Model (1963) to better describe it. In this paper we combined the Fishbein MAUM with fuzzy-set theory to develop a Fuzzy Multi-Attribute Utility Model (FMAUM) to represent the fuzziness and imprecision of consumer decision-making. Multiple regressions are a popular method to determine the weight of MAUM (Dermon & Rouzies, 2005). In order to reflect the imprecise cognition of the fuzzy weights and attribute preference, we use the fuzzy-regression method to build a FMAUM and use automobile purchasing behavior in Taiwan as a case study.

The purpose of this paper is to use this model (FMAUM) to study Taiwanese automobile purchasing behavior in terms of what attributes they use to make a car purchase. Taiwan is a major consumer market for many multinational auto companies. According to the U.S. Department of Commerce, Taiwan was the sixth largest export market in the world for American made passenger cars, and the second largest outlet in East Asia, after Japan. Taiwan was also the ninth largest overseas market for U.S.-made trucks in the first quarter of 2004 (Pan & Koop, 2004). It is important for U.S. marketers to study consumer purchasing behavior in Taiwan and in this case, the auto-buyer behavior before they can effectively compete with other auto firms in Taiwan, or in other markets around the world. And by using FMAUM, U.S. firms can establish a better understanding of the consumer decision-making process when they use product attributes as a specific decision rule for making any purchase decisions.

Linear regression analysis in conjunction with a fuzzy model was first utilized by Tanaka, Uejima and Asai (1982). It is represented as fuzzy linear functions whose parameters are given as fuzzy sets. The fuzzy linear functions are defined by Zadeh's extension principle. In the usual regression model, deviations between the observed values and the estimated values are generally thought to be the result of measurement errors. Tanaka et al (1982) regard these deviations as the fuzziness of the parameters of the system. Thus these deviations are reflected as a linear function with fuzzy parameters. After Tanaka et al's-(1982) research, many researchers applied their fuzzy regression study. Heshmaty and Kandel (1985) use Tanakas' (1982) fuzzy linear regression model (FLRM) applications to forecast sales volume and compare results with a general linear regression model (GLRM). The result demonstrated that FLRM's prediction ability is superior to GLRM's.

Because a fuzzy number can be regarded as a probability distribution, Tanaka (1987) utilized the Zadeh extension principle theory to define the Possibilistic Linear System. He used different methods to analyze and explore the fuzzy parameter. But this can only happen when the independent variable is a crisp value. Sakawa and Yano (2005) proposed that the estimated error between the observed value and estimated value is related to the fuzzy degree of parameter. Bardossy (2005) demonstrated that the problem of fuzzy regression can be formulated as a mathematical programming problem. The linear regression presents several different measures of vagueness: the average vagueness, integral vagueness and maximal vagueness.

Dianond (2005) used Maximum Likelihood Estimators (MLE) to estimate the fuzzy parameter and demonstrate that the MLE can achieve a higher level of fuzzy degree convergency. Savic and Pedrycz (2005) used an enhancement of a minimal vagueness criterion to develop a two-stage construction of a linear regression model. Wang and Ha (2005) used a Minmax parameter estimation method to develop their fuzzy regression model in which both independent variable and dependent variable are fuzzy numbers. Sakawa (1992) used fuzzy measure theory to formulate three types of multiobjective programming problems for obtaining fuzzy linear regression models (FLRM) where both input data and output data are fuzzy numbers.

Moskowitz and Kim (2005) studied different H values and how they can infer the spreads of fuzzy numbers. Chang and Lee (2005) and Change, Lee and Konz (2005) proposed a modification of the FLRM procedure. It allows the range of the parameters to be unrestricted in sign to avoid misinterpreting the data on the approach of Tanaka et al (1982). From the above discussion we know that the FLRM can have two types of variables. In one type, the independent variable is a crisp value, like Tanaka et al's (1982) study. In the other type, all variables are fuzzy numbers, like Sakawa's (1992) study. In the application field the later type is suitable to the fuzzy environment of the real world. Besides, the Sakawa's (1992) FLRM is simple and easy to operate. Therefore, in this paper we use Fishbein's model to describe consumer purchasing behavior and use Sakawa's FLRM to estimate the product attribute fuzzy weight. We call this the Fuzzy Multiple-Attribute Utility Model (FMAUM). The concepts are shown in Figure 1. Overview of Taiwanese Automobile Market Market Situation

There were 4,536,605 cars registered in Taiwan at the end of December 2004. Among those, 275,800 were manufactured in the U.S. This number equaled 6.08% of all registered cars in Taiwan. Of the imports, the U.S. ranked third behind Japan, with 12.57%, and Germany with 6.65%. Table 1 shows the number of cars registered in Taiwan by country of manufacture.

It should be noted that U.S. cars in Taiwan come from two sources. The first is the result of direct investment from auto companies in the U.S., such as Ford Motor Company. The other source is cars imported from the U.S. directly, such as Chrysler and Ford. Toyota also ships models (e.g. Camry) manufactured in the U.S. to Taiwan which, according to the parameters in this paper, would be considered U.S.-made cars. Since cars made in Taiwan possess a 60.42% market share, we will take a closer look at that market situation. Table 2 shows the top five Taiwan-made car brands and their sales volume for the years 2004–2005.

From table 2, we know that Ford's competitiveness in the Taiwanese market is decreasing, while other Japanese auto companies' sales volume has increased gradually, especially Nissan-from 60,342 units in 2005 to 83,405 units in 2004. It should also be noted that in 2004, Ford had the highest expenditures of advertising dollars. Table 3 shows the advertising expenditures of the top five car brands in Taiwan in 2004. Why has Ford's competitiveness in Taiwan decreased in the last two years? Here are some reasons which may explain what happened in the auto market in Taiwan. First, Taiwanese consumers have always liked Japanese products. The preference for Japanese cars is no exception and has further worsened a huge trade deficit for Taiwan. Second, Ford dealers do not aggressively promote their cars in the showroom as do other car companies. Third, Ford's car styles are not as attractive as their competitors. In consumers' eyes, Ford styles are dull and old-fashioned (Car Magazine, 2004). Fourth, competitors have modified their car styles and redesigned their cars in order to attract consumers. For example, Nissan provides 2000cc and 3000cc engine options in its Cefiro model. After the introduction of this car, its market share is more than 40% of the 2000cc-3000cc car market and more than 50% in the above 3000cc car market. Taiwanese consumers chose Cefiro instead of the imported models such as the Toyota Camry, and Corolla, and those of BMW, Volvo, and Mercedes Benz. Cefiro sales reached 33,541 units in 2004, the largest sale volume for all types of cars.

Why do Taiwanese car buyers prefer Cefiro? There are several reasons. First, Nissan's Cefiro is equivalent to what we know here in the U.S. as the Nissan Infinity. Cefiro's luxurious car style and its name represent a higher status and image. Second, Cefiro is equipped with a V6 engine and a micro-controlled air-conditioner. Nissan has successfully persuaded consumers through advertisements that a car with a V6 engine is best. Third, Taiwan Nissan carefully studied the needs and wants of Taiwanese car buyers and designed the Cefiro accordingly. They found the attributes most important to consumers when making purchasing decisions. Many interior decorations and high-priced equipment were added. Items such as wood-like panels, audio phone, VCD, mini-bar, electronic massage seat, power curtains (many of these are unknown to the U.S. market) were added at little or no cost. The price of the car is quite comparable to other manufacturers' models without such accessories. For example, the price for a 2000cc Cefiro is US$20,606 to $24,848. The price for a Toyota Camry without such accessories is US$27,272 to $39,393.

Competitiveness of U.S. Cars in Taiwan

Because of a desire to join the World Trade Organization and pressure from the U.S., Taiwan has increasingly opened its market to foreign products. This, of course, included lowering tariffs on many U.S. automobiles (The Worm Journal, 2004). Thus, one would conclude that the time was right for U.S. automobile companies to sell more of their products in Taiwan. However, Table 2 shows an alarming sign for the U.S. car companies, especially Ford. While other foreign car companies which have a direct investment in Taiwan have increased their sales volume, Ford's sales volume has decreased. In addition, Table 4 shows the number of cars imported from the U.S. has decreased by 40.35% for U.S. brands and 29.59% for the Japanese brands from 2004 to 2007. During the same period, cars imported directly from Japan increased by 108.9%.

Why have cars made in Japan enjoyed an increase of 108.9% from 2004 to 2007 The answer is simple: Taiwanese consumers like made-in-Japan products, especially Japanese cars Although some Japanese cars were made in the U.S. and imported to Taiwan, Taiwanese car buyers still prefer a car made in Japan. They perceive cars made in Japan as having better quality than the ones made in the U.S. Table 5 shows the 2005–2004 top five imported cars' sales volume. From this table, we know that not only the sales volume of imported cars has been decreasing from 2005 to 2004, but while Toyota U.S.A.-remained in the number one position, Chrysler was down from number two in 2005 and 2004 to number four.

A Case Study Background

In this paper we use the FMAUM to study Taiwanese consumers' automobile purchasing behavior when they use car attributes as the purchase decision rule. We focus on the following automobile brands: Nissan, Toyota, Ford, Mitsubishi and Honda, which are all manufactured in Taiwan. These five car brands were also ranked the top five for the last two consecutive years (see Table 2).

The survey was conducted between October 1, 2005, and February 28, 2004. In order to find the attributes consumers used in their purchase decision, we distributed 250 questionnaires to car salespersons, consumers in dealer showrooms, and employees at various companies in Kaohsiung, Taiwan. 169 questionnaires were returned and deemed usable. The response rate was 68%. For the fuzzy number attribute preference portion we distributed 200 questionnaires to consumers who visited dealer showrooms. 126 were returned and deemed usable. The response rate was 63%.

The Attribute Selection

For the attributes which concerned the 169 respondents, we calculated relative frequencies and set a threshold of 0.65. This means that whenever an attribute was chosen by at least 65% of the respondents, we would include this attribute in our study. The cut-off point of 65% was a subjective judgement deemed reasonable for this study. Table 6 shows the car attributes.

Estimated Fuzzy Weight

The first survey results (see Table 6) showed certain car attributes which were shown to the consumers in our second survey. We did not reveal the brand name to the consumers, fearing that these people would be unduly influenced if they knew the car brand. Sakawa's FLRM was then used and, a alpha value from 0.1 to 0.9 was set. The purpose of using Sakawa's FLRM is to simulate how alpha influences the estimated value of parameters (the chosen attributes by 126 respondents). Table 7 shows the estimation results for Model 1 (persons with no car and looking for one with a 1600cc or smaller engine). For the purpose of this paper, only the results for Model 1 are discussed here.

Consumer Purchasing Behavior Analysis

From Table 7 we see that the fuzzy weights (parameters) have overlapped. When alpha = 0.1, the fuzzy weights of the car style and price have overlapped. We call the overlapped area a gray area. This gray area (0.238–0.288) represents the indifference of emphasis on these two attributes by consumers. This demonstrates that the attribute parameter has fuzziness or vagueness in consumers' minds. Besides, the fuzzy parameter spread value of the price is 0.169 (0.389–0.220=0.169) and car style is 0.05 (0.288–0.238=0.05). From this information, we can conclude that first-time car buyers have very different cognition about price weight. This means that the consumers will accept a large price range. But they have clear cognition for the car style.

In summary, the results of the fuzzy weight sensitivity analysis of Model I shows that the viewpoint of respondents who have no car is consistent with the attribute weight of features of a car with an engine smaller than 1600cc. However, the respondents have partial consensus regarding price. When a = 0.3–0.6, the results show that respondents have different viewpoints about the attributes of operation ability, gas consumption and car style, especially gas consumption.

When a consumer purchases a product, his/her preference of a product attribute is a subjective cognition. Based on Fishbein's multiple-attribute utility model and the fuzzy regression model, we construct the Fuzzy Multi-Attribute Utility Model (FMAUM). By using FMAUM, the results in this paper show that the fuzzy weights (parameters) of the attributes have overlapped. The gray area in the attribute weight existed and consumers sometimes expressed their uncertainty of preference towards the attributes. But the FMAUM can reflect the fuzzy cognition of consumers. In this study, the attributes with which consumers are concerned are different under different purchase situations (e.g., having a car already vs. not having a car). Furthermore, when a consumer purchases an automobile in Taiwan, the safety features and the price of the car are the two most important attributes. The traffic accident mortality rate in Taiwan is very high. Many people don't follow the traffic rules very well and often don't keep a safe distance on highways or streets. It is no wonder that the safety features of a car are a major attribute when consumers are making their purchase decision. Price is also an important attribute in this case and therefore, a major reason why the marketing of the Cairo is so successful in the market. The findings from this study can help marketers construct a successful market analysis. First, although we have used consumers in Taiwan to test our FMAUM, any marketing manager can use this model to calculate the fuzzy weights of the attribute and the consensus of the attributes in any market.

Hence, an appropriate marketing strategy can be designed to attract use FMAUM to determine which attributes consumers prefer or which attributes produce a clearer cognition. Then, automobile marketers can emphasize those attributes in their advertisements. Third, by using this model, marketers can determine the attributes consumers prefer most and use this information as a guideline for new product (e.g., car) design. Ford Motor Company an approach to evolution not revolution because an ecological approach can be used to analyze the evolution of any major business. However, a look at how the old-line automobile companies evolved reveals a different time scale than that of almost any new business today. Historically, the evolutionary stages of an established ecosystem like Ford's or GM's often took decades to play out; but now businesses can be born and die in a matter of years. Managers used to focus on directing the action within a particular stage rather than on how to move from one stage to another. Yet transition between stages has currently become a managerial fact of life.

Attracting and encouraging foreign automobile companies to make direct investments and manufacture cars in Taiwan has resulted in the improved quality of Taiwanese manufactured cars. Japanese automobile firms which have direct investments in Taiwan have obviously studied Taiwanese consumer buying behavior. After extensive research, Taiwan Nissan and Taiwan Mitsubishi introduced new car styles (from Japan) and manufacture the cars in Taiwan. This has increased their competitiveness with the imported cars from the U.S. and other countries. Taiwan Nissan even received support from their Japanese headquarters to independently revise their car interior decorations in order to more quickly respond to changing consumer wants and needs in Taiwan.

Managing the supply chain of the Ford Motor Company, one of the world's premier industrial giants ($171 billion revenues in 2004) ranks among the most difficult challenges in global manufacturing Ford manufactures and distributes automobiles in 200 markets across six continents (besides Ford, Lincoln and Mercury, brands include Aston Martin, Land Rover, Mazda and Volvo). North American operations alone involves keeping a network of 19 assembly plants, eight stamping plants, 10 power-train plants and rive forging/casting plants supplied with parts and materials.

Grant E. Belanger, 44, is the man in charge of keeping the machine running as Executive Director of Material Planning and Logistics (MP&L). He has never worked anywhere but Ford since his undergraduate days at the University of Arizona and receiving an MBA in Operations Management from the University of Syracuse. This year marks his 20th anniversary with the company, all of it spent in some aspect of purchasing and supply chain activity (including 3 years in Brazil as the Director of Purchasing for Ford's South American Operations). In 2004, he was brought to headquarters to participate in the revolutionary re-engineering of a supply chain operation that had been essentially unchanged for some four decades.

The magnitude of this undertaking—implementing centralized logistics processes in place of a convoluted spider-web of destination-based supply chains running directly to each individual plant—cannot be overestimated. To do it in two and one-half years, saving 17 percent in costs and improving the reliability of the new network to near 6.0 sigma performance levels, is impressive. But, to have accomplished it while still maintaining on-going operations—without ever having the option to shut down a plant or assembly line, is nothing short of monumental.

The Ford Motor Company is an ever-changing business that tries to stay ahead of its competitors in America and at the global level. Ford's mission is to build great products, strong business and a better world. To accomplish that mission the Ford Company believes that not just quality and cost awareness are the only things that matter, but also a solid relationship with their employees, dealers, suppliers, and every Ford stakeholder With these ideals Ford is proud to be a company with family-based values that allows Ford to have a competitive advantage over its competitors. With this competitive advantage Ford believes that everything they do affects the people they serve from quality and safety of their products to the social and environmental impact on their customers every day lives. The strategy for Ford will be to continue to deliver exciting new products, improve quality and customer satisfaction, improve market share and revenue in all regions, and improve results at all automotive operations. To accomplish this strategy Ford has put pressure on senior leaders to develop a true family culture. To do that the Ford company will have to cultivate a workplace that: attracts and retains the best people, allow them to work at full potential, encourage continuous development and mutual benefit, and promote teamwork while embracing differences and diversity. The keys to Ford's strength are the products. There were forty new products in one year, because of their new realigned vehicle architecture. This allows Ford to produce a greater variety of attractive and competitive vehicles with more shared components and less complexity. But the biggest innovation for Ford is the hybrid. Ford can take advantage of this because they have their own patented hybrid technology and proprietary drive system and electronic controls. Many competitors have not even considered hybrids and when they do Ford will already be a step ahead of them. Currently, Ford offers the Escape Hybrid which has seventy-five percent better fuel economies, especially in the city. Plus, the Escape Hybrid can do anything the regular Escape can do and has the same features.

In the next three years Ford plans on releasing four more hybrids. Ford also has a service for their customers, the Ford Motor Credit Company, which offers many competitive ways for their customers to own Ford vehicles. It's the only product that does not have wheels and it's the finishing piece to Ford's core businesses. Ford North America holds half of Ford's volume worldwide, but their market share was down from 20.5% in 2003 to 19.3% in 2004. Ford is committed in the year 2005 to raise the market share in Europe, South America, and Asia. To do this Ford must still be focused on America and Europe, and start to set up markets in other countries like China that are just starting to make an impact on the world market. Right now North America and Europe account for two-thirds of today's market, but by 2014 it will only account for half of the world markets (Ford motor company, 2004). Ford has made gains in other areas as well; net income where Ford had an improvement of $2.992 billion from 2003, total sales and revenue were up $7.3 billion from 2003, also worldwide vehicle unit sales and European market share were up from 2003 Technology and information systems are very important to the Ford Company. Because of Ford's global scale, information needs to be timely so managers can make important decisions.

With the addition of technology, Ford can make better products at a cheaper price; meanwhile it makes the infrastructure of Ford that much more complicated. Ford tries to introduce new technologies so that environmental and safety features can be added to vehicles before law requires them. One way technology and information systems are helping Ford is in the manufacturing of the vehicles. In established markets such as Europe, North America and Japan, Ford has plants with flexible manufacturing that allows Ford to produce a number of different vehicles in a single location. It enables Ford to add a vehicle line or change over to a new model by reprogramming, rather than retooling, the vast machinery involved. Ford continues to be a leader in automotive technology and information systems, and will continue to forge ahead to create better quality products. As the World's second largest vehicle maker and the World's largest truck producer Ford Motor Company must be able to maintain global market share while keeping the global company connected through company intranets and extranets. Ford Motor Company recently reported a drop in automobile sales of 23 percent. If Ford is going to turn in better numbers in car sales it will have to be an increase in sales not only in America but globally.

While operating a business over multiple continents, in multiple languages, and across multiple time zones Ford is trying to keep the company focused on delivering greater value to its customers to keep the organization and its employees connected over large distances Ford is using a system called room. This technology allows Ford teams to work collaboratively over the Web to connect resources and people. The result of Ford using this system has lead to cost savings in the following areas: time savings, reduced IT costs, and reduced co-location costs. Time is saved using room through increased data sharing and the ability to access documents faster. Replacing many Ford departmental websites with room will reduce IT costs by doing away with IT overhead associated with building and maintaining those websites. Reduced co-location costs will be made through reduced travel costs, video-conferencing costs, and reduced information transmission costs. These reduced costs and the increase in information accessibility are the result of one of the key ways Ford is continuing to compete globally.

Ford is also implementing smaller Enterprise Resource Planning (ERP) systems in regions where they have just recently entered the market. Ford China's IT infrastructure is based on a small ERP from QAD Inc. called Mfg/Pro. This ERP is Ford's standard program for all new markets. Extensions to the standard ERP software make it possible for Ford to comply with foreign practices and government mandated financial statements. Each time a system is deployed in a new market the company gains valuable experience and knowledge that helps the company in future deployments in other new markets. The implementation of a smaller ERP results in quick installation, lower costs than a large ERP, and quick knowledge into the new market. This small ERP system is another factor for Ford's global success.

Nearly from its inception, Ford has been a leader in supply chain practices as part of its innovative assembly line. In the time of Henry Ford, the company directly controlled key material sourcing operations, all the way to mining its own iron ore to ship in its own boats to be rolled into steel in its own mills; meanwhile tire suppliers and the like had their factories nearby.

The company's supply chain of 2005 bears scant resemblance to Henry Ford's. "The days of being 100 percent self-sufficient and capable in today's world of high technology and engineering are gone," Belanger observes. Stark, unremitting global competitiveness has made it imperative that organizations constantly evaluate their use of resources. It is no longer an option to have less-than-optimally productive capital on the books. This has directed pressures, notably at Ford and elsewhere, to streamline the logistics process. Beginning in 2004, when Belanger arrived, the mandate was rationalize a system where it was not uncommon on any day to have 22 different trucks arriving at the same part source to make pickups for 22 different locations. Carriers with half-empty trucks would often cross paths with each other en route to the same plant. "It was very inefficient," Belanger recalls. "What we wanted were fright efficiencies and to improve inventory performance."

To accomplish these objectives, supply chain and logistic processes needed an overhaul. "We knew we had to make some critical changes. MP&L was charged with helping the company improve its time-to-delivery, lean manufacturing and global sourcing goals."

The sheer volume of required support rendered the industry's historic model of self-sufficiency untenable. "It's absolutely necessary to leverage expertise across an organization and with external service providers," says Belanger. To start, the task of supporting plants was split into two networks, one focusing on vehicle assembly plants and the other on power-train plants. "We contracted with two different proven logistics providers with two very different technological approaches," recounts Belanger. "Each worked hard to redesign and manage our networks. With their help, we changed our approach from a destination-based network to an origin-based network with increased visibility."

Adopting a consumer mindset as well as one of environmental and social responsibility requires leadership. We need leaders who can make informed business decisions that will make our company better able to meet customer needs and increase shareholder value, as well as honor commitments to the world in which we live. Change like that is easy to talk about but difficult to implement. It will take nothing less than a massive shift in culture to create new leadership DNA. Nothing short of revolution will do. And that is where our Leadership Development Center enters. Our vision is to be the center for the revolution, developing Ford Motor Company leaders to change the world. Our mission is to accelerate transformation to a consumer-and share-holder-driven business, to accelerate the identification and development of leadership talent, and to drive the company's mission, vision, and values deep into its culture.

How can we do that? We've developed a series of leadership programs centered on these core principles:

1. Adopt a transformational mindset.

2. Use action learning—learning by doing, leading, and teaching.

3. Leverage the power of e-tools.

4. Integrate work and life, what I call "total leadership."

5. Generate business impact.

The company's main impetus for securitization is having an alternative source of funds. Besides investor capacity, Boss her said, the company focuses on "making sure that we have in-house core competency from legal, tax, systems, administrative, treasury—all those perspectives. We have to have the capability to securitize as much of the balance sheet as possible," he added. These same initiatives prompted Ford to add, for the first time, a D class to its most recent issue in February. The $46 million class was partially retained and was rated "BB." Large deals have also always been part of the strategy— the company's first securitization, in 2005, consisted of two back-to-back, public, auto loan transactions totaling $5 billion.

Swat Analysis

Ford Motor Company (Ford) is one of the largest automotive manufacturers in the world. The company's automotive vehicle brands include Aston Martin, Ford, Jaguar, Land Rover, Lincoln, Mazda, Mercury and Volvo. The company manufactures and distributes automobiles in 200 markets across six continents. The Ford Asia, Africa and Ford Mazda operations recorded strong performance in fiscal 2005. Strong Ford Asia, Africa and Ford Mazda could prove to be a significant revenue and profit driver in the coming years. Intense competition from Japanese companies, however, could lead to further deterioration in the North American operations of Ford.

Strengths Weaknesses

Strong Ford Asia, Africa and Ford Mazda operations

Growing Ford Europe and PAG operations

Profitable financial services division

Weakening North American automotive operations

Tarnished brand image

Large unfunded pension and other obligations

Opportunities Threats

The way forward plan

Hybrid vehicles

Opportunities in India and China

Rising raw material prices

Increasing competition

Low capital spending

Strengths

Strong Ford Asia, Africa and Ford Mazda operations The Ford Asia, Africa and Ford Mazda operations recorded strong performance in fiscal 2005. Revenues from Ford Asia, Africa and Ford Mazda reached $8,245 million in 2005, up 18.5% over 2004. More importantly, this segment recorded an income before taxes of $297 million in fiscal 2005, up from $82 million in fiscal 2004. Strong Ford Asia, Africa and Ford Mazda could prove to be a significant revenue and profit driver in the coming years.

Growing Ford Europe and PAG the Ford Europe and Premier Automotive Group (PAG) recorded strong revenue growth in fiscal 2005. The Ford Europe and PAG primarily include the sale of Ford brand vehicles in Europe and Turkey as well as sale of PAG brand vehicles (Volvo, Jaguar, Land Rover and Aston Martin). Revenues from Ford Europe and PAG reached $60,258 million in 2005, up 11.3% over 2004. Ford Europe and PAG accounted for 34% of total revenues. Growing Ford Europe and PAG has enabled the company to offset revenue decline in the Americas division.

The Profitable financial services division, of the Ford Motor Credit, is largely responsible for keeping the company afloat. In fiscal 2005, the financial services division has recorded income before taxes of $5,891 million, up from $5,008 million in fiscal 2004. In contrast, the automotive division recorded loss before taxes of $3,895 million in fiscal 2005, up from $155 million in fiscal 2004. As a result, the company was able to record a net profit of $2,024 million in fiscal 2005. In recent years, the problems of automotive division have adversely affected the credit rating of the financial services division. This has forced the financial services division to resort to securitizing of retail auto loans, auto leases and lines of credit to car dealers on its books for raising money. As a result, revenues of this division have fallen in recent years. Yet financial services division continues to remain profitable.

Weaknesses

Weakening North American automotive operations Ford's automotive operations in North America recorded a weak performance in fiscal 2005. Revenues from automotive operations in North America fell by 2.4% to approximately $80,600 million in fiscal 2005. Furthermore, automotive operations in North America recorded a loss before taxes of $2,500 million in fiscal 2005, as compared to an income before taxes of $684 million in fiscal 2004.

The weakening of automotive operations in North America is due to competition from Japanese companies and a market shift away from fuel-guzzling light trucks such as sports utility vehicles toward more fuel efficient vehicles. Ford relies more on truck sales than other vehicle manufacturers. Truck sales accounted for 67.2% of its US vehicle sales, whereas in case of most other vehicle manufacturers, truck sales account for only 56% of total vehicle sales. Stagnating truck sales in the US, on account of high fuel prices, has hurt Ford more than the others. Japanese competitors such as Toyota have also taken market share away from Ford. The company's share of the US light vehicle market, the largest in North America, has fallen from 19.3% in fiscal 2004 to 18.2% in fiscal 2005. Ford's automotive operations in North America accounted for about 45.5% of total revenues in fiscal 2005. Any continued weakening of automotive operations in North America would adversely affect the financial and market position of the company.

Tarnished brand image—The brand image of Ford has been tarnished owing to persistent product recalls. In 2000, the US Department of Transportation investigated 271 tire tread separations largely involving Ford's sports utility vehicle, Explorer. Ford spent $2.1 billion in 2001 replacing 13 million tires made by Bridgestone/Firestone. In 2001, Ford recalled new Escape sports utility vehicle five times in four months owing to quality issues During January 2005, Ford recalled about 792,000 pickup trucks and sport utility vehicles because of a fire risk from overheating of the speed control switch. According to a leading consumer magazine, an eight year old Toyota is as reliable as a three year old Ford with 54 problems per 100 vehicles. Tarnished brand image has negatively impacted Ford's sales in the US.

Large unfunded pension and other obligations Ford have significant unfunded pension, health care and life insurance obligations. By the end of 2005, Ford's total pension obligations, including the US and non-US plans, totaled $74,595 million, while pension assets (US and non-US) totaled $63,784 million, which resulted in unfunded pension obligations of $10,811 million. Total health care and life insurance obligations of Ford stood at $39,274 million at the end of 2005, while the plan assets stood at $6,497 million, resulting in unfunded health care and life insurance obligations of $32,777 million. Unfunded pension, health care and life insurance obligations would negatively impact the cash flow position of the company.

CHAPTER 3

▼

METHODOLOGY

Industry research—Questionnaire survey

Restructuring and change have characterized the car industry in the past decade. Over-capacity, increasing customer requirements, tougher environmental legislation and rapid technology development are among the most important factors behind this development. To stay competitive, car manufacturers and suppliers therefore continuously need to improve their performance (see McIvor et al., 2004) regarding production (e.g. delivery precision, quality, and cost) and product development (e.g. time, cost, innovativeness). As a consequence, several trends (here defined as general changes over time within the industry) concerning sourcing strategies and supplier relations can be identified. In this first part of the article, important trends are identified based on available research and literature and then, in the following sections, these trends are analyzed further by comparisons with empirical data.

Regarding the car industry as a whole, there is an evident change towards more global operations (Sturgeon, 2004; Getaway and Ghadar, 2000). With a global presence, car manufacturers and suppliers may, for instance, increase their production volumes and thereby benefit from economies of scale. Several car manufacturers have therefore recently merged with or acquired other car manufacturers. The merger between Daimler and Chrysler, Ford's acquisitions of Volvo and Jaguar, and GM's acquisition of Saab are only a few examples. The same applies to suppliers where a few actors (e.g. Delphi and Lear Corporation) have become dominant players mainly through acquisitions of smaller suppliers (Lewis and Wright, 2004; McIvor et al., 2004).

Proposal (trend)
P1 Increasing importance of key performance criteria (e.g. delivery precision, quality, cost)
P2 Product life-cycles become shorter
P3 Production and product development activities become more globalized
P4 Outsourcing is increasing
P5 Companies reduce their supply base
P6 Product development time is decreasing
P7 Suppliers account for an increasing share of product development resources
P8 Use of JIT-deliveries is increasing

Also the vertical relations, i.e. between car manufacturers and suppliers, have changed in the past decades. For instance, several researchers have referred to the trend of increasing outsourcing (see e.g. Mercer, 1995; McIvor et al., 2004). By outsourcing certain activities to specialized suppliers, companies can focus on those products and activities that they are distinctively good at (Venkatesan, 1992). This specialization, enabling a reduction of the capital base, implies improved return on invested capital (Quinn and Hilmer, 2005) and possibilities to benefit from economies of scale. However, outsourcing means that important activities are placed outside the boundaries of the firm (Richardson, 2005). Hence, extended co-operation between car manufacturers and suppliers is needed to ensure efficient co-ordination of these activities (Dubois, 2005). However, co-ordination of activities demands vast resources, and many companies therefore strive to reduce their supply bases (Cousins, 2004), i.e. the number of suppliers to the company.

	North American	European	Asian	Total
Car manufacturers	2	7	2	11
First tier suppliers	4	9	3	16

When it comes to products, the most important drivers for changes are decreasing product life cycles and increasing product customization and variety (see e.g. Bullinger, 2005; Hartley, 2004; Pine, 2005; Åhlström and Westbrook, 2004). Shorter product life-cycles demand cost reductions, reduced development time and faster production ramp-ups (see e.g. Lamming, 2005; Almgren, 2004).

At the same time, product customization complicates cost efficiency since the volume per product variant is reduced. To handle this problem, car manufacturers increasingly use product platforms and modularization. By using a global platform for several product models, production volume may be increased, at the same time as product variants can be created by modifications of modules (see e.g. Ulrich and Tung, 2005; Baldwin and Clark, 2004). An illustrative example is Volkswagen's group-wide product platforms (see Wilhelm, 2004).

| | Car manufacturers | | | | | Suppliers | | | | |
	1988	←	1998	→	2003	1988	←	1998	←	2003
Delivery precision	3.0	**	4.0	*	4.4	3.2	**	4.3	**	4.9
Quality	3.5	*	4.7		5.0	4.2		4.6	*	4.8
Product cost	3.6		4.5		4.6	3.9	**	4.9	*	4.7
Customized products	2.4	*	3.5	*	4.1	3.2		3.7		4.1
Product related services	2.5	*	3.5	*	4.2	2.2	**	3.3	**	4.1
Development time	3.2	*	4.1		4.4	3.1	**	4.1	*	4.6
Development cost	3.3	*	4.0		4.3	3.1	**	4.0	**	4.4
Product innovation	3.0	*	3.9		4.2	3.2	**	4.3	*	4.7

Notes:
*Significant increase between 1988-1998 or 1998-2000 = $p < 5$ per cent);
**significant increase between 1988-1998 or 1998-2000 = $p < 1$ per cent)
Scale from 1 = not important to 5 = very important

The use of modules for product customization will have implications for the manufacture and assembly of products. Although the basic modules are the same, creating a large number of variants makes it difficult and costly to keep all of them in stock. The use of sequenced just-in-time deliveries from module suppliers has therefore become more frequent (see Mercer, 1995). Short delivery time then becomes an important criterion which, in turn, demands that suppliers are located close to the customers' assembly plants (Millington et al., 2004). For example, many suppliers have established local assembly units in supplier parks. There, product modules are customized and then delivered just-in-sequence to the car manufacturer's assembly line. This demand on proximity in module supply is another important factor behind the globalization of suppliers' production activities (Helper et al., 2004).

	1988	1998	2003[c]
Car manufacturers[a]	7.4	5.8	5.7
Suppliers[b]	6.5	5.0	4.1

Notes:
[a] Significant difference between 1988-1998 (p < 5 per cent)
[b] Significant difference between 1988-1998 and 1998-2003 (p < 1 per cent)
[c] Significant difference between car manufacturers and suppliers (p < 1 per cent)

Also product development has been affected by the changing conditions within the car industry. For example, as stated above, shorter product life cycles demand shorter development time. Further, outsourcing and (organizational) specialization, in combination with modularization, has created new conditions for product development. Supplier involvement in product development is, for instance, made easier when products are split into modules (see e.g. Fine and Whitney, 2005). By involving suppliers in product development, customer firms may take advantage of the suppliers' knowledge regarding product development and production. Thereby, development time and cost may be reduced (Clark, 2005). Supplier involvement has therefore attracted an increasing interest over the past decade (see e.g. Wynstra et al., 2004). However, supplier involvement is a complex task, implying that companies become more dependent on their suppliers (Nishiguchi, 2005). As a consequence, closer relationships are needed and car manufacturers have to focus their resources on a few strategically important suppliers (Kamath and Liker, 2005). This is a factor explaining the supply base reduction mentioned above.

Taken together, there is no doubt that the car industry is going through a period of change and restructuring. To summarize the sourcing-related trends outlined above, eight proposals have been formulated in Table I.

	Production			Product development		
	1988	1998	2003	1988	1998	2003
Car manufacturers	14.9	15.7	15.9	2.6	2.1	3.0
Suppliers[a]	5.8	12.2	15.0	2.6	5.0	5.9

Note:
[a] Significiant increase between 1988-1998-2003 for production (p < 1 per cent) and for product development (p < 5 per cent)

The identified trends are often referred to among practitioners, in the media and by researchers. It is, however, difficult to find references providing hard facts supporting (or rejecting) these trends. Many authors in fact routinely refer to these sourcing trends, which implies a risk that they become "stylized facts" that are not critically reviewed. Hence, there is a need for a more comprehensive, and critical, review of these sourcing-related trends. This article aims at providing quantitative data regarding the outlined sourcing-related trends and, further, to compare these results with existing research. The aim is also to investigate whether there are differences between car manufacturers and first tier suppliers. Further, it can be assumed that relationships exist between some of the identified trends.

	1988[b]	1998[c]	2003[b]
Car manufacturers	61.7	63.7	65.7
Suppliers[a]	41.6	46.4	50.6

Notes:
[a] Significant difference between 1998-2003 ($p < 1$ per cent)
[b] Significant difference between car manufacturers and suppliers ($p < 5$ per cent)
[c] Significant difference between car manufacturers and suppliers ($p < 1$ per cent)

The remainder of the article is structured as follows. In the next section, the research method is outlined and explained. Then, the results are presented, analyzed and discussed. Finally, conclusions are drawn and suggestions for further research are given.

Research method

The empirical research in this article is based on a survey of car manufacturers and first tier suppliers. In order to enable comparisons between these two categories, they were given identical questionnaires. The questions were formulated in a way that would enable investigation of the proposals shown in Table I. However, the referred proposals and trends were not explicitly addressed in order to avoid some bias due to "stylized facts". To enable an analysis of the development over time, the respondents were asked to provide estimates regarding the years 1988, 2004 and 2003, respectively. The study was performed during 2004, implying that the most recent company data available would be from 2004. Further, it was assumed that, during the ten-year period between 1988 and 2004, most companies participating in the study would have introduced new models. Thereby, they would also have had opportunities to fundamentally change their operations.

To go ten years back in time was also considered to be enough to capture some of the "pre-lean" conditions (in the West). Ten years was, however, considered to be too long a time for predictions about the future. Five years from 2004, resulting in predictions concerning the year 2003, was assumed to be a reasonable time. Further, to enable the respondents to use company records and forecasts as a basis for their answers, the questions were mainly of a quantitative nature (i.e. company figures and Likert-scales).

	1988-1998[b] (%)	1998-2003 (%)
Car manufacturers	−25	−16
Suppliers[a]	18	−16

Notes:
[a] Significant difference between 1988-1998 and 1998-2003 ($p < 5$ per cent)
[b] Significant difference between car manufacturers and suppliers ($p < 5$ per cent)

Several companies, especially among the suppliers, may have activities outside the automotive sector. All companies were therefore asked to provide data concerning their automotive business only. Further, all companies were asked to answer the questions with regard to their own situation and their own products. However, the issue concerning division of product development resources (between car manufacturers, first and second tier suppliers respectively) was an exception since all companies were asked to answer exactly the same question. Further, comparisons between car manufacturers and suppliers need to be examined carefully since there is a risk that they perceive exactly the same phenomenon in different ways.

This risk is, however, assumed to be less pronounced here. Because, when all respondents answered exactly the same question regarding product development resources, no significant differences were found between car manufacturers and suppliers.

	1988	1998	2003[c]
Car manufacturers[a]	4.7	3.3	2.6
Suppliers[b]	3.6	2.5	1.8

Notes:
[a] Significant changes between 1988-1998 (p < 5 per cent) and 1998-2003 (p < 1 per cent)
[b] Significant changes between 1988-1998 (p < 1 per cent) and 1998-2003 (p < 1 per cent)
[c] The difference between car manufacturers and suppliers is significant (p < 5 per cent)

The sample of companies originates from Automotive News Europe (2004, 2004) where the largest (in terms of turnover) car manufacturers and first tier suppliers were listed. Small car manufacturers with low volumes (e.g. Morgan and Rolls-Royce) were not added to the sample since the characteristics of their operations differ greatly from high volume manufacturers' operations. Among first tier suppliers, large companies were assumed to have most influence over the car manufacturers' operations (providing a large share of the purchased value). These companies were also assumed to have more influence over the supplier structure as a whole than smaller suppliers have. These lists were therefore regarded to be a useful basis for the study. In total, the sample included 32 car manufacturers and 92 first tier suppliers.

In most cases where one company owns several different car manufacturers or brands (for example, Audi, Skoda and Seat that are all owned by Volkswagen), the survey was sent to each of these manufacturers.

	1988	1998	2003
Car manufacturers[a]	76.7	59.8	50.0
1st tier supplier[a]	17.7	30.6	38.2
2nd tier supplier[b]	5.6	9.6	11.8

Notes:
[a] Significant differences between 1988-1998-2003 (p < 1 per cent)
[b] Significant differences between 1988-1998 (p < 1 per cent) and 1998-2003 (p < 5 per cent)

In March 2004 the survey was mailed to purchasing, development and company executives. Unless the companies declined participation, several reminders were sent to those who did not answer the questionnaire. In November 2004, when the data collection phase was ended, 27 companies had answered the survey. This gives a response rate of 21.8 per cent. The limited sample size will, however, have implications for the possibilities to draw conclusions from the data. It is important to note that larger differences between groups can be found, while the possibilities of detecting smaller differences are limited (see Verma and Goodale, 1995). In other words, differences that do exist (e.g. between car manufacturers and suppliers), but are small, may not be detected because of the limited sample size.

Proposals regarding sourcing related trends in the car industry	Car manufacturers		First tier suppliers	
	1988-1998	1998-2003	1988-1998	1998-2003
P1 – Increasing importance of key performance criteria	Supported on a general level Partially supported on a detailed level			
P2 – Product life cycles become shorter	Supported	Not supported	Supported	Supported
P3 – Production and product development activities become more globalized	Not supported	Not supported	Supported	Supported
P4 – Outsourcing is increasing	Not supported	Not supported	Not supported	Supported
P5 – Companies reduce their supply bases	Supported	Supported	Not supported	Supported
P6 – Product development time is decreasing	Supported	Supported	Supported	Supported
P7 – Suppliers account for an increasing share of product development resources	Supported	Supported	Supported	Supported
P8 – Use of JIT deliveries is increasing	Supported	Supported	Supported	Supported

Consumer Research—Questionnaire survey

A total of 11 car manufacturers and 16 first tier suppliers, (see Table II) answered the questionnaire. A majority of the answers are from Europe, but also North American and Asian companies are represented in the study. The number of responses does not enable comparisons between countries. However, the bias towards European companies called for a check for regional differences. No significant differences were found, except among first tier suppliers regarding the division of product development resources. This is further discussed in the following section. Furthermore, both small and large car manufacturers are represented in each geographical category. The same applies to the suppliers with a yearly turnover ranging from $500 million to

$6 billion. Hence, both small and large companies are represented, although the very largest "mega suppliers" did not participate in the study. The suppliers that responded are active within areas such as interior, exterior, chassis, engine and transmission, thereby covering the technology areas represented by the suppliers in the original sample.

The analyses of the data have mainly been focused on similarities (or differences) and correlations. Histogram plots showed, however, that most variables were not normally distributed. Moreover, the number of responses implies that the variables can be regarded as discrete (especially when using sub-groups of data). Therefore, parametric tests like the t-test could not be used. Instead, the non-parametric Mann-Whitney's test was used for independent variables and Wilcoxon's test for dependent variables (e.g. comparisons between different years). Correspondingly, for the correlation analyses, the Pearson-correlation was replaced with Spearman. The chosen methods are more conservative than the t-test and the Pearson-correlation, which means that the analyses of the data have been relatively more restrictive.

All research designs have their limitations, the one used here being no exception. As described above, however, precautions have been taken to interpret data in a careful and conservative manner. The results presented in this article should be seen in the light of the general scarcity of fact-based evidence regarding current trends in the car industry. So, even though the number of responding companies in the data sample is limited, the results can help to further develop the picture.

Results

This section presents the results of the survey investigating sourcing trends in the car industry. The section is structured according to the eight proposals presented in the introduction. In addition, correlations between some specific variables are tested. Explanations and discussions of the results are presented in the following section:

Increasing importance of key performance criteria

As a consequence of overcapacity, intense technology development and increasing (and diverging) customer requirements, the first proposal (P1) stated that the importance of key performance criteria is increasing. To assess how the car manufacturers and suppliers actually perceive different criteria, they were asked to specify the importance of eight performance criteria for their company's competitive strength in 1988, 2004 and 2003. The results are shown in Table III.

When considering the car manufacturers' and suppliers' responses taken together (not shown in Table III), all performance criteria were expected to be more important in 2003 than in 1988. Furthermore, all criteria but product cost increased in importance between 2004 and 2003. It is the car manufacturers that do not expect product cost to be more important in 2003 than in 2004. Moreover, product cost is the only criterion that the car manufacturers did not regard as more important in 2004 compared to 1988. In fact, the car manufacturers only expect delivery precision, customized products and product related services to become increasingly important between 1988 and 2003.

These three criteria also showed the largest significant increase during this period of time. Suppliers, on the other hand, consider more performance criteria to be increasingly important. As seen in Table III, customized products is the only criterion that suppliers do not expect to be more important in 2003 than in 2004, while both customized products and quality were seen as equally important in 2004 as in 1988. Considering the relatively high rankings in Table III, however, it is clear that most performance criteria are regarded as important for a majority of the companies:

It was argued in the introduction that product life cycles become shorter. This was also stated in the second proposal. To assess if this really is the case, the car manufacturers and first tier suppliers were asked to estimate the average life-cycle lengths for own products introduced in 1988, 2004 and 2003. The results are shown in Table IV.

The results show that both car manufacturers and suppliers expect a shorter life cycle for a product introduced in 2004 compared to one introduced in 1988. However, only suppliers expect to reduce product life cycles even further until 2003. For 1988 and 2004, there were no significant differences between car manufacturers and suppliers regarding product life cycles. In 2003, however, the suppliers' expected product life cycles are significantly shorter than the car manufacturers'.

Globalization has been measured as geographical dispersion of production and product development activities. To test if globalization is increasing, as suggested by the third proposal (P3), the respondents were asked to estimate the number of countries in which they have, or will have, production and product development activities in 1988, 2004 and 2003. The results are shown in Table V. The results clearly show that the car manufacturers are not changing their geographical dispersion of production or product development activities. The suppliers have, on the other hand, significantly increased the number of countries in which they undertake these activities (see Table V). On average, they actually expect to almost triple the number of countries where they have production activities and more than double the number for product development.

Outsourcing is increasing

Organizational specialization was referred to in the introduction as one way for companies to respond to increasing competition. It was, therefore, proposed that the degree of outsourcing is increasing (P4). To assess whether this is really the case, the respondents were asked to estimate the cost of purchased materials as share of total turnover. The results are shown in Table VI.

Somewhat surprisingly, the results show that the car manufacturers have not significantly increased their degree of outsourcing, and do not intend to do so. Neither did the suppliers increase their cost of purchased materials as share of turnover between 1988 and 2004. However, they expect a significant increase between 2004 and 2003. The results in Table VI also show that there are significant differences between the car manufacturers' and suppliers' degrees of outsourcing. The car manufacturers thus outsource more than suppliers in terms of purchased materials in relation to turnover, but the suppliers intend to increase their share. By reducing the number of suppliers, companies can invest more resources in improving their relationships with the remaining suppliers. It was therefore proposed that companies are reducing their supply bases (P5). Table VII shows how the respondents estimated the change in number of suppliers to their companies between 1988 and 2004 and between 2004 and 2003 respectively.

The results in Table VII show that the car manufacturers have, on average, reduced the number of suppliers by one quarter between 1988 and 2004. Over the same period of time, the first tier suppliers actually increased their supply bases by on average 18 per cent. However, between 2004 and 2003, both car manufacturers and suppliers expect to reduce their number of suppliers.

Correlations between product life cycle, outsourcing and supply base So far, the results have shown that the car manufacturers and first tier suppliers expect different product life-cycle length, degree of outsourcing and supply bases. In the following, correlations between these variables are tested.

It can be assumed that the companies expecting the shortest product life cycles will, to handle this challenge, have the highest degree of outsourcing. However, no significant correlations were found between length of product life cycle and degree of outsourcing. The same applies to the car manufacturers' changes over time (1988 to 2004 and 2004 to 2003). However, the suppliers' expected change in product life cycle length between 2004 and 2003 is negatively correlated with their expected change in degree of outsourcing (-0.623, $p = 0.042$). This means that the suppliers that intend to shorten their product life-cycles also plan to increase their degree of outsourcing.

The degree of outsourcing is, however, not the only measure of companies' utilization of suppliers to improve performance. Close co-operation with a few suppliers may be a way of achieving shorter product life-cycles. The data was, therefore, tested for a relation between changes in the number of suppliers and in the length of product life-cycles. However, no significant correlations between these two variables were found.

There is also a possible relationship between the car manufacturers' and first tier suppliers' degrees of outsourcing and their number of suppliers, as well as between changes in these variables. In order to reduce transaction costs and improve co-operation, companies may, for instance, outsource more to fewer suppliers. Only one correlation was, however, found between changes in these variables. A negative correlation (-0.672, $p = 0.047$) exists between the car manufacturers' change in number of suppliers between 1988 and 2004 and their expected change in degree of outsourcing between 2004 and 2003. This means that the manufacturers that have reduced their number of suppliers intend to increase their outsourcing in the near future.

To assess whether car manufacturers and suppliers are reducing their product development times, as proposed in the introduction (P6), the respondents were asked to estimate the average development time for own products introduced in 1988, 2004 and 2003. The results are shown in Table VIII.

It is clear that both car manufacturers and suppliers have shortened their average development times over the past ten years and that they expect to continue this reduction until 2003. In total, the respondents expect reductions of 45–50 per cent between 1988 and 2003. Further, the results show a significant difference in development time between car manufacturers and suppliers in 2003. On average, the suppliers then expect to have a 30 per cent shorter development time than the car manufacturers: Suppliers account for an increasing share of product development resources.

As referred to in the introduction, it has been observed that suppliers to an increasing extent are becoming involved in the car manufacturers' product development work. It was therefore proposed that suppliers account for an increasing share of the total development resources (P7). In order to modulate the picture further, all respondents were asked to estimate car manufacturers', first tier suppliers' and second tier suppliers' share of the total product development resources in 1988, 2004 and 2003. The question, thus, concerned the general dispersion of development resources. The results are shown in Table IX.

As shown in Table IX, the car manufacturers' share is estimated to decrease from about three-quarters in 1988 to half of the total product development resources in 2003. The suppliers are consequently increasing their share of product development resources. Both first and second tier suppliers are expected to more than double their relative shares between 1988 and 2003. On average, the car manufacturers and first tier suppliers gave almost identical answers about this division of development resources in the past and the future. Thus, no significant differences were found between the two categories.

However, a geographical comparison showed major differences between the Asian and European suppliers' answers. Compared to the Asian suppliers, the European suppliers estimated that the first tier suppliers' shares of product development resources were significantly larger during all the investigated years ($p < 5$ per cent). Their respective views on the car manufacturers' shares of product development resources did also differ. The Asian suppliers estimated car manufacturers to have a significantly larger share of product development resources. Their views on the second tier suppliers' shares were similar.

Correlation between development time and share of development resources so far, it is evident that product development time has decreased and that suppliers are taking an increasing responsibility for product development. According to the arguments put forward in the introduction, there may be a relation between reduced development time and a higher degree of supplier involvement (measured as share of total product development resources).

For the analysis, the car manufacturers' and first tier suppliers' shares of product development were correlated with their respective development times. These analyses were done for each of the years 1988, 2004 and 2003 and for the changes between these years. The results show, however, no significant correlation between a high degree of supplier involvement in product development and a short development time. The above-suggested relation between the suppliers' share of product development and development time is therefore not supported. There is, however, one interesting exception. The respondents' estimations for 2003 in fact give a strong negative correlation (– 0.80, p = 0.006) between the car manufacturers' share of product development and development time. This indicates that car manufacturers that plan to do a large share of the development work in-house expect to have the shortest development times:

Use of JIT-deliveries is increasing.

It was proposed in the introduction that companies increasingly use inbound just-in-time deliveries (P8). To assess the use of JIT-deliveries, the car manufacturers and first tier suppliers were asked to estimate the share of purchased materials delivered to their companies according to JIT-principles in 1988, 2004 and 2003. The results are shown in Table X.

Table X clearly shows that both car manufacturers and suppliers will continue to increase their share of inbound JIT-deliveries. On average, the respondents expect an increase by approximately 30 per cent between 2004 and 2003. Furthermore, the results also show that car manufacturers' and suppliers' inbound JIT-deliveries are at a similar level.

Correlation between JIT-deliveries, number of suppliers and degree of outsourcing In line with the arguments in the introduction, it can be assumed that the increasing use of JIT-deliveries is related to reduced supply bases, and to some extent, more outsourcing. The data was, therefore, tested for correlations between these variables. No significant correlations were, however, found between these variables, neither for the car manufacturers nor for the first tier suppliers. The same applies to changes over the years for the first tier suppliers (1988, 2004, 2003) and for the car manufacturers between 1988 and 2004. However, a positive correlation (0.790, p = 0.020) was found between the car manufacturers' intentions of increasing the share of inbound JIT-deliveries and reducing the number of suppliers between 2004 and 2003. This correlation indicates that the car manufacturers expect to receive more modules and systems according to JIT-principles from fewer first tier suppliers.

Analysis and findings in relation to existing research

How, then, do these results relate to the trends proposed in the introduction? This section synthesizes the survey results and relates them to the outlined propositions. Existing research is also used for explaining and discussing the survey results, which are presented in Table XI.

The starting point for this article was that increasing competition forces companies in the car industry to improve their performance. Regarding certain key performance criteria (see P1 in Table XI), the survey results support this belief on a general level only (see Table III). The car manufacturers considered all criteria but product cost to be more important in 2004 compared to 1988, while only delivery precision, customized products and product related services are believed to be even more important in 2003. The suppliers perceived all criteria except quality and customized products to be more important in 2004 than in 1988. The latter insignificance may however be explained by the differing importance of variety in the suppliers' products. Another explanation for the varying importance of the criteria is the dynamics among order-winning, qualifying and less important criteria, as explained by Slack et al. (2004). Based on Hill (2005), Slack et al. argue that criteria that were once order-winners turn into qualifiers as new criteria become order-winners and so forth. This dynamic indicates that the competition in the car industry is not only increasing, but also changing in nature.

Particularly interesting, is the fact that both car manufacturers and suppliers expect a significantly increasing importance of product related services. This implies that car manufacturers will take an increasing responsibility for leasing, financing, insurance, repairs etc. Already today we have seen the beginning of this development and this may fundamentally alter car manufacturers' business strategies and operations (Wise and Baumgartner, 2004). A similar development may be outlined for suppliers of systems or modules since car manufacturers' requirements are rapidly transferred down the supply chain.

In line with other research (see e.g. Bullinger, 2005; Lamming, 2005), the present survey results indicate that product life cycles are becoming shorter. Both the car manufacturers and the suppliers expect life cycles to be shorter for products introduced in 2004 compared to those introduced in 1988 (see P2 in Table XI). However, the car manufacturers do not expect life-cycles to be shorter for products introduced in 2003 compared to those introduced in

2004. A plausible explanation is that car manufacturers, due to the huge investments required for launching new products (Almgren, 2004), have reached a minimum life-cycle length. More frequent, but partial, product renewals can instead be achieved by letting suppliers upgrade their components or systems. First, tier suppliers have better conditions than their customers for exchanging existing products more frequently since they develop products in parallel and in different phases with several car manufacturers. This could be one of the reasons why suppliers expect to have significantly shorter life-cycles for their products, compared to the car manufacturers.

Globalization was outlined as one of the most influential trends in the car industry. According to the present survey results, however, car manufacturers do not disperse their production and product development activities into more countries (see P3 in Table XI). Considering the overcapacity in the industry, utilization of existing knowledge and capital intensive resources are reasonable explanations for this situation. Instead, globalization seems to be achieved through other means, e.g. through the use of global platforms that form the basis for many different car models produced in existing plants. Honda's and Volkswagen's global platforms are typical examples of this (Sugiura, 2005; Automotive News Europe, 2001).

Suppliers, on the other hand, do globalize their production and product development activities (see P3 in Table XI). This difference between car manufacturers and suppliers may be explained by suppliers having acquired local component suppliers in strive to become systems and module suppliers. Geographical dispersion is also, in many cases, a consequence of the suppliers' need of having a close relation with each customer (Dyer, 2005). One clear example here is the local assembly units that suppliers establish in supplier parks close to their customers' final assembly plants (Sako and Warburton, 2004; Mercer, 1995), or their use of guest engineers in product development projects (Twigg and Slack, 2004). Since most suppliers have more than one customer, geographical dispersion of both production and product development activities is necessary. Thus, a decreasing difference between car manufacturers and suppliers can be seen in this respect (see Table V).

Considering the degree of outsourcing, it was found that neither the car manufacturers nor the suppliers have increased the cost of purchased materials as share of turnover between 1988 and 2004 (see P5 in Table XI). Thus the survey results do not support the general belief that the degree of outsourcing is increasing (see e.g. Mercer, 1995; McIvor et al., 2004). But why is this so? Concerning the car manufacturers, the results show that their current level of outsourcing, on average, lies above 60 per cent. If outsourcing even more, they may risk losing control over the car as a complete system, or losing competence and resources that they define as core (see Quinn and Hilmer, 2005). Although the relative economic value of purchased materials has not increased, however, car manufacturers may still have outsourced more responsibility. Assembly of modules, for instance, accounts for a relatively small share of total materials costs while implying a major difference in the suppliers' responsibility (Sako and Warburton, 2004). This clearly shows that the picture of the "increasing outsourcing" trend is more multifaceted than generally discussed.

Similar arguments can be used when discussing the suppliers' constant level of outsourcing between 1988 and 2004. However, their situation is slightly different. Many suppliers have in recent years focused on horizontal growth through mergers, acquisitions and forward integration (McIvor et al., 2004). It is, therefore, likely that they have "inherited" activities that they regard as non-core. They may now instead focus on internal restructuring and therefore outsource some of their non-core activities. This explains the suppliers' expected increase in outsourcing in the near future (see P4 in Table XI).

A related issue is the size of supply bases. Maintaining supplier relations is costly, and many companies, therefore, strive to reduce their supply bases (Cousins, 2004). This is important when considering the close relationships needed for JIT-deliveries and co-operation with suppliers in product development. The survey results show that the car manufacturers have reduced their supply bases and plan even further reductions (see P5 in Table XI). The suppliers did, on the other hand, increase their number of suppliers. It is reasonable to assume that module and systems suppliers have "inherited" component suppliers when the car manufacturers restructured their supply bases. Furthermore, suppliers' globalization of production may also have contributed to the establishment of relations with local suppliers, e.g. for logistical reasons. According to the results of the study, however, the suppliers intend to follow the same path as the car manufacturers, and reduce their number of suppliers in the near future.

The last three propositions are fully supported by survey results (see P6-P8 in Table XI). Thereby, the trends concerning shorter product development time, suppliers' increasing share of product development resources, and an increasing share of JIT-deliveries to both car manufacturers and first tier suppliers are confirmed. Many other researchers argue that relations between car manufacturers and suppliers are becoming closer (see e.g. Lamming, 2005;

Dyer and Ouchi, 2005). These survey results, therefore, support car manufacturers' decreasing supply bases and suppliers' globalization. Taken together, it thus seems as if the car industry is moving towards closer relations between car manufacturers and a rather small number of suppliers that supply complete systems and modules. Through local establishments, these suppliers will develop their modules and deliver them, just-in-time, to a larger extent than today.

A final comment concerns the differences between car manufacturers and suppliers at a general level. It seems as if suppliers in some cases are lagging behind car manufacturers in the adherence to a trend. Regarding level of outsourcing (P4) and supply base reduction (P5), for instance, the results indicate that first tier suppliers undertake the same changes as car manufacturers, but in subsequent periods. A reasonable explanation is that car manufacturers have adopted principles that then extend upwards in the supply chain. Such dispersion of working principles is greatly enhanced in closely integrated supply chains. While suppliers are seen as an increasingly important source of product and process innovations (Gadde and Håkansson, 2001), there may, of course, exist cases where working principles flow downstream. However, no examples of this were found in the survey results.

Questionnaire survey results

EContent spoke with Bob Schwarzwalder, manager of library systems and information research for the Ford Motor Company, to help sort through some of the issues, challenges, and opportunities that exist in this arena. Bob is no stranger to readers of EContent, its sister publication ONLINE, or to other industry watchers. He was the Technophile columnist for Database, now EContent, for several years and has written and spoken widely on information systems engineering, electronic publishing, data mining, and knowledge management. In addition, Bob serves on the advisory boards for several publishers and database producers. An early and ardent proponent and practitioner of buyer/vendor alliances, he has long advocated codevelopment of information systems and content-sharing-especially in the business-to-business space.

EC: I noticed, in reviewing the industry literature on this subject, that there does seem to be a preponderance of articles on the troubles or dissatisfactions between vendors and buyers. Or is that being pessimistic?

Bob: While I think that's right—that much of the literature points out the frustrations—I regard that as just a sign that selling electronic information is a very new thing, and a lot of what we're experiencing are inevitable start-up pains—a sort of discovery. It's new. There are a lot of concerns that people have, but this is just a natural stage in evolution.

EC: I'd like to explore this area on a very fundamental level. For starters, what is it that content buyers really want?

Bob: There really are a lot of different people buying information out there. I can speak from our own experiences here at Ford and those people I talk to from the corporate enterprise, but these experiences probably are not generalizable, because we each have some advantages and disadvantages that others don't have.

But I do think you can say that when you look at buying electronic information, most people want to integrate it into some sort of preexisting structure. People will buy their first information product and may want to just use a desktop system or client on their own, but, for the most part, the big market is for folks who have some sort of existing system and want something that can be integrated. Often, we also want a customization of the product in some sense, and we're willing to pay for it. But sometimes, the seller really doesn't have that ability, and that's a problem.

Buyers are also looking for a low cost per use—not necessarily a cheap product—but one that on a cost-per-use basis is economical or at least reasonable. There are many products out there that are so highly niched and expensive that they are cost-prohibitive.

A buyer is really interested in something that's going to fill a gap in their coverage. Again, the big buyers are the folks who already have a number of products and are looking for something that really fills that gap. Now there are exceptions to that, but if you are the fourth news service to come calling, you're probably going to be met a lot less enthusiastically by the buyer. The buyer wants something that really fulfills some important need. For example, Ford has very little in the way of criticism of English literature, but we really have no need; we're not likely prospects for the MLA Bibliography vendors.

The last thing I would add from the buyer perspective (and this is particularly true of large corporations like ours) is that the process has to be contractually acceptable. This is often a hard point for sellers to understand. For example, you may encounter a minor information product with a low cost, and the vendor will have a 15-page document that needs to be signed off and agreed to, to the point where it's absolutely nonsensical.

EC: How about training and support? Is it important to buyers?

Bob: I think it is, and at various levels. The technical support is a bare minimum. This can become important in areas like security because we're developing a lot of different nuances to firewalls and security. A lot of times, you need a technical support that is fairly sophisticated just to get access to the content. Since security systems change—sometimes frequently—you need to have a good response time to that, or the system will totally shut you down.

EC: What about payment options?

Bob: Having various kinds of payment options is important. One of the real problems I've run into is the site license issue. A lot of content vendors began selling to universities, and there, the site license model makes a lot of sense. For a multinational company, it makes no sense at all. I couldn't tell you the number of sites Ford has. I tried to find that out once, and I couldn't find anyone in the corporation who knew! What constitutes a site for us varies a lot. We can have a couple of people in a remote location working in concert with a government agency or with a different company somewhere else in the world, and it really doesn't make sense to call that a "site". You may get those kinds of payment options where they can only sell a product to you by site, and there is really no way to comply. So, the buyer wants flexibility in all things, but especially in payment plans and licensing.

EC: Why aren't buyers getting what they want? What intrinsic characteristics or methods of operation, or what external circumstances or forces, are thwarting them?

Bob: From the buyer perspective, it's always because of inflexible vendors! (Laughter)

Seriously, I think often what you have is a lack of fit. In terms of business practices, I just mentioned the licensing models. The terms and conditions whereby a seller is doing business may just not jive with the way that your company does business. This is the "contractually acceptable" piece. I think there is the perception on the part of sellers of information systems—actually all of us have this certain hubris—that what we do is very important. If you're a seller for Reuters or Dow Jones, or Dialog, or STN, or anybody, you happen to think your system is a big deal, and so, you think, of course people will modify their rules if they need to—they will modify them for us. You get a large corporation that may buy millions of tons of sheet metal per year—buying access to a database is nothing to them. You're not going to convince your purchasing people to modify a rule that exists for buying sheet metal and glass and widgets and wheels, so that you can buy a database. So there is really often no flexibility on the buy side, and that can be very difficult to convey to a seller.

There can also be a real lack of fit into the network environment. The development of information products has really been driven by those products having a unique interface—a proprietary interface. Once the buyers become used to that, they're more prone to buy that vendor's next product. But if that product doesn't fit with the buyer's local system, if it's a standalone product—and most are, from the corporate network perspective—it makes it harder for people to go into it and use it.

Buyers who are inexperienced or inflexible can also be a problem, because they come into this situation with very unrealistic expectations. On the library side, there seems to be this illusion that making a profit is some sort of capital crime—that if an information seller actually wants to make money on a product, this makes them evil!

Finally, the vast proliferation of information products and ways in which each product is packaged, and the highly dynamic nature of the information marketplace, has caused some buyers to become overwhelmed by the number of options and experience a kind of "buyer's paralysis." This has also created an uncertainty that forces people to retain paper copies of things and, in a sense, dilutes the money that could go into buying the electronic version.

EC: Let's talk about the factors that favor the buyer's position. What do buyers do particularly well or what resources could help them get closer to their goals?

Bob: One, money! Since the buyers are the ones who are ultimately funding the effort, they have an inherent leverage over the whole process. They also have the ability to network within their organizations to create ad hoc internal consortia to fund enterprise-wide contracts. Two, an understanding of the information needs of their organization, and three, an ability to help tailor the product to ensure use

All of these are reasons why a partnership between the seller and the buyer makes so much sense. To the degree that an information product serves an organization's needs well, it is a success for both the buyer and the seller. For the seller, this ensures future funding. For the buyer—who may have had to stretch to get funding for the product—it establishes credibility and helps solidify that buyer's role within the organization.

EC: Who is doing the buying? Do you see some kind of profile emerging in the corporate enterprise?

Bob: Yes, I see more consolidation in this area. Part of it is that enterprise-wide licenses are driving out the "piecemeal" kinds of arrangements. While certain vendors have done a very good job of contacting end-users and selling multiple copies of content across an enterprise, $his approach is increasingly being viewed by the corporation as being inefficient, bureaucratic, and more costly. Enterprise-wide buys that enable the organization to deal with someone higher up the chain, and not the sales representatives, are becoming more common.

EC: Let's turn our attention to the supply side. What do vendors really want?

Bob: I think first and foremost, they want money. (Laughter)

This can be deleterious to a longer-term relationship at times. There is a very mixed bag with vendors. There are the people who are just fly-by-night, looking for a quick sell, and are not too smart about it, and there are those who are looking for long-term customers. A lot of the idea behind branding a product is that it really establishes a presence for the product and reflects the vendor's desire to establish a long-term relationship.

I think the more-enlightened sellers really want the buyer's collaboration to help tailor their product to the buyer's environment, so that it is really successful-really used. They understand that by seeing how the product is used, it can give them new ideas for how to improve the product, how to sell it, or how to tailor it to new markets.

EC: We talked a bit about the inflexibility of both buyers and vendors. What other intrinsic factors or methods of operation work against the vendor?

Bob: I think the biggest problem with vendors is that they often really don't appreciate or understand their customers' needs and wants. There are certain things that are largely disconnects: the models for selling and licensing that can be problematic, a lack of understanding of corporate purchasing realities, the branding of products, which can cause problems in integrating content.

Also, in the corporate world, we encounter sellers who profess a real fear of copyright infringement, and sometimes these infringement fears are way overblown. For instance, I recently spoke with someone who expressed alarm over the possibility that a user would download his content and send it off to everyone on the Internet. Now, this person sells industry standards, and I don't know if you've ever read any industry standards, but they are the most boring pieces of information. The idea that someone would download one and send it to everyone on the Internet is ludicrous—it makes no sense at all.

I'm not saying that copyright is not something to be zealously guarded, but on the other hand, you have to take reasonable steps, and sometimes the steps people take are wholly unreasonable.

EC: Let's talk about the fee-versus-free-versus-hybrid issue. Do you think that people no longer believe "you get what you pay for"? How has this affected the vendor?

Bob: There are a lot of information companies who came into being under this whole dot com craze. The model has been this: they get some venture capital. They establish enough of a claim to go public. Part of establishing a claim is to get some high-profile customers. They will often virtually give away access to their system to a company like Ford, so that when they go IPO, they can say, "Our customers include Ford," and blah, blah, blah. So you're getting vendors who have high-value content, who, in order to get the eyeballs, and make the claims and get this IPO money, are virtually giving their content away, so it's not just going onto Yahoo! or something. We're talking about people with specialized, high-value content that also are sort of complicating this fee-versus-free thing.

I think the marketplace is going to wash those folks out. I don't think this is a long-term phenomenon; what is a long-term phenomenon is this whole idea of simply finding information. If you chart this out as a commercial space, and you think about it in terms of niche space—in the biological sense that there are certain roles and there are certain potentials to do certain things—the idea of just retrieving information is an area that's getting very crowded out. If the only thing a company does is retrieval, it is in trouble.

There has been a lot of discussion about educating the user that you get what you pay for, and free information is worth what you pay for it, but you're not going to win with that argument. For one thing, there is a lot of good information that is free. For another, you're asking for a level of discernment by the user that is just not realistic. I think the clever users are learning how to add more value to their systems so it's not just pull-retrieval on demand—but its push, or it's integrated, or there is a level of complexity or nuance to it that you can't get elsewhere. That's how the successful products are differentiating themselves in the marketplace—and it's wholly necessary.

EC: So those are some areas in which vendors have been improving their position: in customizing their products and developing more of the push technologies …

Bob: Oh, yes. Look at a company like Factiva, for instance. They have a lot going for them. If you look at how they develop within an intranet, they really go in and tailor applications, so they're giving buyers a total package that has a lot of advantages that you couldn't get for free—the currency, the complexity, the scope, and the fit. That's why they are successful in the marketplace.

EC: What about external circumstances, such as technology, competition, or policy that affect the vendor's position?

Bob: One of the things that both works for and against content vendors is the Web itself and the technologies associated with it. The Web really created an environment where you don't need middlemen. For the middlemen, of course, this is a bad thing. However, a lot of vendors were able to enter the marketplace directly instead of working through companies like Dialog, because the technologies enabled them to reach a vast and diverse marketplace relatively cheaply and easily—a tremendous advantage. Also, a lot of technologies are developing that are lowering the cost to produce the information. The methodologies are just becoming better.

Now there is also a disadvantage here in that if you lower the barriers to entry, then basically anybody can become an information vendor. That's become fairly widespread. The primary resources are being sold, resold, and sold yet again, and there are all kinds of people selling the same kinds of things because it is really cheap to get into the business.

EC: We've touched on some of the ways in which buyers and vendors can cooperate, such as working together to customize and integrate content and develop satisfactory licensing and payment agreements. What other thoughts do you have on facilitating more in the way of win-win relations between the two?

Bob: I think the first thing for buyers and vendors to do is to really get together and try to speak honestly and openly about their needs and work out their problems. Being somewhat creative about what is sold, how it's sold, and where the revenues come from can help create options for a deal where a deal might not have been created before.

The most profitable thing for all parties is to see this as a partnership that will enable them to develop approaches jointly. That helps the seller learn about the kind of audience he or she is dealing with, learn about their needs, and explore options for delivering the information. It allows the buyer to basically get something that is really valuable to him or her. Ultimately, the only way for both buyer and seller to be successful is if the end-user finds the result valuable.

EC: Do you see those kinds of relationships developing sometime soon?

Bob: I do. Clearly, in the future, we're also going to see some consolidation of the market as a lot of players' exit the market and stronger ones emerge.

EC: I'd like to talk a moment about life since The Technophile. You had said in your farewell column that it was time for you to move on, because you had expressed what you wanted to express. Has anything come up in the interim that you would like to point out?

Bob: I've certainly pontificated enough about what people are doing wrong and what they need to do right. I think that my position now affords me an ability to try some new approaches and new technologies. My hope is that I can actually respond to some of my own criticisms because for too long I've talked about what people are not doing and now it's my chance to try to do some of it.

I don't think I no longer have anything to say, but my hope is that in a year or so, I can start saying some new things and talking about new ideas and approaches and roll those out, rather than just questioning why we aren't doing something new. That's what I'm up to these days. But there are some very exciting things happening; these are exciting times.

CHAPTER 4

▼

DISCUSSION

Supply chain management system
Finding the Best Fit

The Ford Motor Company finds itself in a dynamic business environment where new technologies and practices offer the potential to alter in a significant way the landscape in which it operates. Henry Ford was in his time an innovator in offering 'cars for the masses'. He introduced to the car industry methods and systems innovative in their day. Ford needs once again to forge new paths to ensure future competitive advantage.

Executives at Ford have been considering the 'Direct Model' created by Dell Computer Corporation and finds that there is considerable appeal. Dell has been able to speed up inventory velocity such that there is only eleven days of inventory on hand. This has led to an inventory turnover rate of thirty times per annum. This achievement, termed by Michael Dell 'Virtual Integration' has been achieved by blurring the line between supplier, Dell and client, to the extent that third party service staff are often thought, by clients, to be Dell's own staff.

In order to see how congruent the Dell model is to Fords' business we need to examine the similarities and differences between the two companies. This will allow us to gain some insight as to whether virtual integration could work at Ford.

At Ford Motors we: Cars are consumer items.*Computers are a consumer item. Suppliers are often located close to manufacturing facilities.Ford maintains close locational links with suppliers. Number of suppliers is small.*Ford is working to build relationships with a limited number of strategic suppliers. Ford's customers range from large corporations, to government institutions, to the consumer.*Dell's clients range from large corporations, to government institutions, to the consumer.

Ford and information technology

Key to Dells' strategy is their policy of outsourcing all manufacture. Dell acts merely as the assembler and packager. The company is able to pick and choose from the range of industry leading components, allowing other manufacturers to make the investments in leading edge technology. The suppliers manufacture their, essentially generic, products for many customers and therefore are economically independent of them and also have little difficulty in meeting the JIT (just in time) requirements of Dell.

Since the Ford Motor Company's incorporation by Henry Ford in 1903, its strategic focus has remained on automobile design and manufacturing. Up until 1970, competition was from the two other manufacturers making up the Big Three Automakers; General Motors and Chrysler. However, starting in the 1970's, foreign competition, mostly from Toyota and Honda, eventually lead to overcapacity within the industry. As more and more developing and industrial nations encouraged development into the automobile industry, overcapacity in the automobile markets reached an estimated 20 million vehicles. In 1995, in an effort to reduce cost and increase efficiency, Ford developed a restructuring plan called Ford 2000 that was to focus on globalizing corporate organizations and taking advantage of the economies of scale in purchasing and manufacturing by consolidating the North America, European, and international automobile operations. Ford 2000 also called for a complete reengineering of several key company processes including Order to Delivery (OTD) and Ford Production System (FPS). One of the primary strategic goals of Ford 2000 was to decrease OTD from 60+ days to less than 15.

To help overcome information constraints in Ford's new global approach, they launched a company-wide Intranet in mid-2005. In addition, Ford further expanded upon that system to include business-to-business (B2B) capacity by January 2004 which also comprised the Automotive Network Exchange (ANX). Ford's public Internet site went live in 1995. Internet usage exploded, and by mid-2004, Ford's website was getting more than 1 million hits per day. During this revolutionary time, Ford was honored as the most improved automaker in the 2004 JD Power Initial Quality Study; listed as number 4 overall behind Honda, Toyota, and Nissan.

With an eye on the global market, each automobile manufacturer was looking to expand their global reach. By mid-2004, Chrysler merged with Daimler-Benz. Several months later, Ford announced that it would acquire Sweden's Volvo. Rumors of other mergers began to surface. By the end of 2004, Ford surpassed Chrysler in profit per vehicle ($1770) while total profit hit $6.9 billion.

In 2004, Jack Nasser, who was second in charge since Ford 2000 was initiated, took over as CEO. Mr. Nasser had a reputation of being a cost cutter, a capable leader, and a senior manager focused on increasing shareholder value.

Today, the Ford Motor Company is the second largest industrial corporation in the world operating in 200 countries around the globe. Ford employs more than 350,000 and revenues exceed $144 billion annually. Since incorporation, Ford has produced over 260 million vehicles.

Issues

Ford needs to address a couple of issues in trying to determine which information technology strategy will work best for supplier interaction as well as with their current engineering projects.

1. Ford's current supplier base:

    a. Ford recently decreased their supplier base to have a closer and more long-term relationship with fewer suppliers called 'Tier 1' suppliers. These suppliers provide Ford with complete vehicle subsystems. The Tier 1 suppliers work with multiple Tier 2 suppliers who provide the components that make up the vehicle subsystems.

    b. The Tier 1 suppliers do not have the capital to invest in the new technologies that Ford seeks to get into. However, the Tier 1 suppliers do have fairly solid IT capabilities, but these capabilities severely drop when dealing with the Tier 2 suppliers.

2. Purchasing organization:

   a. Ford's purchasing department is independent of the product development area. However, purchasing has a strong dominance over the product design price negotiations because "a very slim reduction in purchasing cost could result in very significant savings" for the company.

   b. Dell's vertical integration has these areas working very closely together. Could Ford also successfully merge these two areas?

3. Forecasting within the Ford 2000 projects:

   a. Two key initiatives under the Ford 2000 project are the Ford Production System (FPS) and Order to Delivery (OTD). The FPS project was geared at making Ford manufacturing operations leaner, more responsive, and more efficient by focusing on continuously flowing material through using vehicle in-process storage units and proper assembly order sequence. The OTD project was started to reduce the order time from 60+ days down to only 15.

   b. The accuracy of Ford's forecasting is an integral step in being able to maintain the continuous flow of materials from suppliers as well as being able to turn the vehicles around within 15 days. This is the first time that Ford had ever involved the dealers with forecasting the customer demand.

Ford has at one time, both notable similarities and striking differences in terms of their relationship with suppliers. Many Ford components such as tyres, windscreen wipers, and electrical components are sourced from large suppliers who supply the same components to other companies. These products are well suited to a closer integration of supply—virtual integration.

On the other hand, a very large proportion of Ford components are custom made for Ford. Tier one suppliers of custom components such as body panels, seats and engine components are heavily dependent on Ford and other large carmakers. These suppliers second tier suppliers, who in turn also have suppliers. If virtual integration is to succeed with these components every company along the value chain right back to the raw materials would need to be involved. This would be a very difficult and complex network to coordinate.

Fords' history is a factor to be considered, their longevity and size in the industry gives them a tremendous degree of influence when compared with Dell, a relative newcomer to business and whilst a large buyer of components, not so influential on trends and technology. The disadvantage may be that this stature may make it hard to bring their very large organisation and supplier network along the road to virtual integration.

The dealer network must be considered. The dealers carry a very limited range of products, which they hold in stock. If Ford decides to carry the Direct Model towards the end consumer they need to ask whether they need a dealer network and in what form. The possibility of disintermediation needs to be examined. Alternative forms, that use the existing network may be viable, for example, the dealer might be used to postpone the final form until the point of customer order. This might be the fitting of audio equipment, air conditioning or interior trim customisation. This would enable more consumers to benefit from the vast possible range of options, as well as, at the same time reducing the factory lead-time for manufacture.

Further discussion of the present findings

While no contract between Allan Nevis, Columbia University and Ford Motor Company appears to exist, the company's files do contain correspondence and a draft copy of a proposed agreement, submitted to Ford by Columbia University in October 1951. These records indicate a healthy tension between the company and the author. Clearly, it was a major coup to have the enthusiastic interest and commitment of a Pulitzer Prize-winning historian to write a history of Henry Ford and Ford Motor Company. Just as clearly, Nevis was excited at the idea of working on a project that had enormous societal relevance and interest. He wanted the full cooperation of the company in conducting his research, but he also wanted to ensure that his academic integrity could never be called into question. The company wanted to cooperate, but there was concern about how the history might be interpreted. The following points summarize the Columbia University proposal for addressing the relationship:

Standards: Nevis would agree in writing that "the history and biography shall be a thorough, scholarly and literarily attractive work, sympathetic in character to Henry Ford and the Ford family; provided, however, that the work shall meet standards of critical scholarship and that the requirement of sympathetic treatment shall not in any way operate to limit the attainment of such standards."

Limited "veto" power: In the event of a disagreement over content, Ford Motor Company could exercise "veto" power over specific points, or it could express its views in a footnote or an appendix—with one very important exception: " … no veto power shall exist or be exercised with respect to statements concerned exclusively with the policies, ideas, acts or personal relationships of Mr. Ford as an individual." Arbitration process: Recognizing that this concept of "veto power" might lead to serious disagreement between the company and the author, the draft contract called for an arbitration process for settling disputes. The proposed arbitration committee would consist entirely of representatives from Columbia University (including Columbia's president, the dean of the Graduate Faculties and the dean of the School of Business).

Ownership and royalties: Nevis would have "complete control over the contents of the work and the property of the manuscript," including copyright. Publication royalties would go to Columbia University.

Compensation: The only compensation Nevis would receive would be his salary from Columbia University. Ford was to provide financial support to Columbia to cover salaries, expenses and overhead for Nevis and two research assistants. Access: Ford would make its archival records available to Nevis and his research assistants, and would work to obtain the consent of the estates of Henry Ford and Edsel Ford for access to their records.

Ultimately, the funding was provided through grants to Columbia University from the Ford Motor Company Fund, a nonprofit corporation organized in 1949. A later, and apparently final, version of the agreement for the book project was described in an exchange of letters in November 1951 between Columbia University's president and the vice president of the Ford Fund. The letters stated that Professor Nevis would create a two-volume history and biography, under the aegis of Columbia University; identified a total amount for the undertaking (to be paid over a four-year period through a series of grants); stated that Columbia University would receive the publication royalties; and promised that the Ford Fund would receive a copy of the manuscript at least three months prior to publication.

By choosing to fund the project through the Ford Fund, a separate legal entity that by its charter could not impose controls over a grant project of this sort, the company appears to have relinquished any influence over Nevis' scholarly interpretations. Later correspondence does not indicate any effort by

Ford to "veto" any part of Nevis' work. As it happens, the arrangement proposed by Columbia University was probably unworkable—there were too many opportunities for conflicting interpretations. It took a leap of faith on both sides—Ford, on the one hand, and Nevis and Columbia, on the other—to make the project work.

Ford Motor Company's Information Systems

An information system consists of input, processing, output, and feedback. With these activates the information system helps to produce the information that associations need to get better decision-making, problem solving, controlling operations, and creating new products or services.

The information systems can assist a business in that they contain important information about an exacting client, place, or event that get place in the organization or the environment nearby it. Information systems are not as important for smaller stores as it is for the larger corporations.

A Management Information system (MIS) can be distinct as an organized assembly of resources and procedures required to collect and process data and deal out information for use in decision-making. It serves the management echelon of the organization, providing managers with reports and, in some cases, with on-line access to the organization's current performance and historical records. Generally, a MIS is dependent on fundamental transaction processing or operational systems for their data. It is important to differentiate between information and an operational system. MIS as an information system will gather and collate data and distribute information from the current operational systems like the depot systems. Management information is a tool to be used and will never replace common sense. It is supplemented by other management tools and not used in separation. A single management report from a MIS is never used to make a policy decision. A number of reports over a period are used to establish a propensity and that is used as a basis for investigation.

Problem Identification of The Management Information Systems of Ford Advances in information technology and perceived dissatisfaction with MIS performance is leading users to take over their own systems development work. This does not mean an end to the MIS department, but a staff rather than line responsibility will be required as users become the dominant developer of information systems. For a successful transition, HRD will be expected to operate as a change agent helping both groups adjusts to their new roles.

The introduction of microcomputers into the workplace during the 1980's ushered in a new era which is having a profound effect on organizations. More specifically, users are taking greater control for systems development in their organization. This change requires user departments to prepare for new responsibilities and the Management Information Systems (MIS) department to adapt to a new role and purpose within the organization. Furthermore, the Human Resource Department (HRD) needs to help manage the conversion from an MIS dominated to a user controlled environment. (Allen, 1987)

Technology Factors

Expensive computers, and the need to have a FORD employee program the computer, centralized computing in one department where the mainframe was the centerpiece of the operation. In the 1970s the development of smaller computer systems (e.g. minicomputers) made it possible for user departments, which had specialized functions such as research or development, to acquire some of their own computer equipment. In fact mid sized and small computers are often referred to as departmental computers to signify their use by user departments rather than CMIS. Nonetheless, in terms of the total volume of computing being conducted, FORD easily remained the major information systems organization during the 1970s.

One of the obvious changes that end user independence precipitates is a decentralization of the information system function. In addition to the affordable price of hardware, which places computers within the reach of many user departments, the efficiency of PC's relative to mainframes is an important consideration for a cost conscience government. This economic consideration also favors acceleration in user departments justifying their own hardware. States are also anticipating further technological and managerial changes which are indicative of a strong user's orientation—greater use of powerful small computer systems, growth in user computing and an increase in computer networking and data sharing. (Bennis, 1967)

Organizational Factors

The primary issue is the performance of FORD as perceived by users. A survey by The Partnership for Research in Information Systems Management or

PRISM illustrates the type of disenchantment users experience with FORD. The survey found that 75% of users, who had acquired their own systems, cite unsatisfactory performance by FORD as the most important factor in wanting their own system. These users also justify their independent systems on the grounds that they can produce systems more quickly and better tailored to their needs than FORD. Furthermore, functional managers perceive FORD as unresponsive to their needs. Adding to the Duties of User Departments

   The most pronounced change for user departments is the opportunity to develop their own information systems. As Allen observes, users are in a better position to evaluate and acquire their own information systems than CMIS. Specific information systems functions will fall to departmental staff with more specialized training in the discipline—tasks familiar to FORD such as planning strategic departmental information systems, determining information needs, obtaining hardware and software within guidelines established by CMIS, assessing whether systems are in conformity with regulations and policies, and evaluating the exposure of risk from information systems failure. Restructuring the Role of FORD, a change in FORD duties appears inevitable. (Gauch, 1992)

Planning and Standards Development

FORD is the most reasonable place to locate the information planning and control responsibility for the organization as a whole.

Technical Leadership

The background and experience of the professional FORD staff is particularly well suited to perform the technology tracking function within organizations.

User Support

The change in user department FORD roles places a greater responsibility on FORD in the area of user support. The establishment and maintenance of local area networks represents another area for user support.

Computer Operations

A viable data center operating the mainframe and ancillary equipment will remain an integral part of FORD. It is noted that there is a controversy over the future of the mainframe and visualizes its eventual replacement by PCs. In the future, PCs will be capable of running the applications that are now run on the mainframe. However, for the immediate future, mainframes will be part of the information architecture of large organizations.

Systems Development and Maintenance

Although there will be a decrease in systems development work, the manpower required for systems maintenance is expected to increase. On the other hand it creates a personnel problem within FORD since systems maintenance is perceived by FORD professionals as de-motivating, low level work.

The Situation in State Governments

Most states have drawn up an overan statewide plan for information systems. Furthermore, progress in preparing privacy and security plans within state governments are minimal.

The growing importance of user training in state governments is reflected in the percentage of FORD resources devoted to this function. (Currie, 2004)

Managing the Transition

As users take control of their own systems and MIS decentralization proceeds, employees in FORD become less sure of their futures. User departments will be staffed with people, possessing not only technical skills in their functional area of responsibility, but with a proficiency in a second discipline, MIS. Managerial issues also need to be addressed including overcoming resistance on the part of FORD to the decentralization of the MIS function and changing traditionally defined MIS jobs. As user departments assume responsibility for MIS professionals, it is appropriate to ask whether MIS personnel can be handled the same way non-MIS personnel are supervised or should departmental administrators be prepared to modify their management style? The motivational patterns are similar for MIS and non-MIS personnel within each of three occupational groups (Clerical, technical and managerial).

Discussion's Conclusion
The HRD Role

To initiate the process, HRD needs to communicate with FORD and user departments to ascertain the extent to which the MIS role is changing. A working group with representation from all involved departments and HRD create, problem solve and manage an action plan. Determining the type and number of MIS positions required for each Department. Creating job descriptions and a salary structure for new positions, matching current staffing versus needs and identifying areas of under and over staffing. Developing training and development plans. Beyond the technical training, a plan to "socialize" individuals who transfer to a new department need to be considered. As the program evolves HRD should also be sensitive to the need to hold team building exercises within a department when appropriate. Discussing with current staff their interest in a career change, in many cases individuals lack an understanding of the career choices within their present position and, even if they choose not to take on new responsibilities, they will profit from an understanding of their current options. Individuals opting for a career change need to be fully informed regarding the training needed and sources for the training (e.g., in-house or through outside organizations)

Instituting and monitoring individual plans. No matter how carefully thought out a plan may be, it does not guarantee success. HRD should retain contact with transferred individuals and depending on circumstances; HRD may wish to sponsor workshops which address problems or successful outcomes. (Henderson, 1986) HRD should retain contact with transferred individuals and depending on circumstances; HRD may wish to sponsor workshops which address problems or successful outcomes.

It is clear that in state governments the transition from a FORD controlled environment to a user dominated environment is occurring. An early step in this process is for HRD to join forces with FORD and the user departments. In a joint enterprise HRD can be instrumental in identifying career paths and opportunities for both FORD professionals and user personnel.

Ford's Most Famous Failure

It would surely be difficult to point out at one single reason for the failure of Ford Edsel (Genat, 2004). Marketing is a complex issue, so we have to overview what Ford Edsel and its failure was all about? At the end of my overview, I have suggested some points related to good marketing that may have made Edsel a success.

Back in 1956, Ford Motor Company realized that there was a void in their selections of mid-size automobiles.

While Chevrolet owners could 'move up' to a Buick, Pontiac or Oldsmobile and Dodge owners could advance to a Plymouth or Chrysler, Ford buyers were looking at Mercury alone.

The perception was that Ford was losing customers to other manufacturers when the time came to trade-up. In order to correct the problem, Ford instituted plans for an entirely new car division, and an entirely new car. The design of the car was to be completely unique and distinguishable from any angle. And the promotional build-up of the car would be like nothing else.

The 1958 Edsel came in two sizes, the big and the bigger. The 'Senior' series cars were the Citation and Corsair models. They were built on the large Mercury-based frame. The 'Junior' series cars were the Rangers, Pacers, and station wagons Bermuda, Villager and Roundup, which were built on the smaller Ford-based frame.One of the most talked about feature was the 'tele-touch' shifter, which controlled the automatic transmission selection electronically from push buttons in the center of the steering wheel hub. Many other Edsel-original ideas are still found in today's cars. The car was referred to as the 'E' car from its inception. The name 'Edsel' was bestowed by Special Products Division General Manager Richard Krafve, after reviewing a list of nearly 8,000 suggestions from their advertising firm, Ford employees, and even a renowned poet.

After a massive promotional campaign, which included multi-page 'teaser' ads in major national magazines, some two and a half million Americans poured into Edsel dealerships on 'E-Day', September 4, 1957. But it was quickly apparent that few cars were actually being sold (Olsen, 2002). The public expectation was much higher than the car could live up to, and sales reflected the disappointment. There was a combination of other factors that led to the name 'Edsel' becoming synonymous with 'failure'. By the time the first Edsel hit the showroom, the country was in a recession.

Trading-up means that a brand is moving towards a higher and bigger range. It does not imply that the brand itself becomes bigger in size. At that time, the car-buying habits had turned toward smaller and more fuel-efficient cars. Edsel's styling was radical, and not broadly appealing.

On the assembly line, Edsel was run between Fords or Mercury's, causing the assembler to have to interrupt his routine and sometimes forget to install some parts.

The Edsel also suffered from parts that wouldn't fit together correctly. Because of problems with suppliers, many of the early cars arrived at the dealerships with parts missing, and many dealers were poorly equipped to replace the parts or add on accessories. Ford Vice President Robert McNamara offered little support to the Edsel Division. The Edsel was more expensive than other comparable cars, and the price of the loaded, top-of-the-line models that were first on the showroom floor scared many buyers. There was no owner loyalty to count on. And, finally, it had a funny name. The Edsel Division was in a death spiral. The more cars that failed to sell, the more dealers dropped their Edsel franchise. The more dealers that folded, the more the public was afraid to buy the car. After three model years and just 110,847 Edsels later, Ford Motor Company threw in the towel, and went about trying to forget about the whole ordeal. Today less than 6000 Edsels survive, and very surprisingly, each one is a cherished classic.

As a marketer, I'd look at the product, price, point of sale, promotion (Kotler, 2002), as well as the geographic, psychographic and demographic target market of Edsel.

Here, the point of sale does not matter that much. But I have to consider that I am the marketer, and not the manufacturer, so I could've done less to alter the product. I should admit that when people awaited an aero-dynamic, fuel efficient, and compact car, Edsel was the exact opposite. This would've led to an entirely different strategy in the promotional campaign against the one that was adopted, since this car surely was not for the masses. This also meant that the pricing should've also been revised. A rock solid service guarantee may have increased the sales, since the parts of Edsel were a problem. But in my opinion, this car should've been restricted to the elite since it wasn't for the masses. This high-pricing strategy might've been successful, for fewer cars would've been manageable for the Ford Company, and the cost could've been recovered by the high price. But I should admit that these are all assumptions.

CHAPTER 5

▼

RECOMMENDATIONS

Improvement Tactics Employed by Organizations

The term tactics is usually viewed as a short-term strategy and one which can be employed with minimal preparation and one which can also be summarily suspended. Below we shall list the tactics that firms have employed and follow with a number of illustrations.

The tactics are:

- Solicit ideas for improvement from employees.

- Encourage and develop teams to identify and solve problems.

- Encourage team development for performing operations and service activities resulting in participative leadership.

- Benchmark every major activity in the organization to ensure that it is done in the most efficient and effective way.

- Utilize process management techniques to improve customer service and reduce cycle time.

- Develop and train customer staff to be entrepreneurial and innovative so as to find ways to improve customer service.

- Implement improvements in the organization so that it can qualify as an ISO 9000 supplier.

The above list includes most of the successful tactics employed by organizations in their quest to become more or remain competitive in their respective industries. Since tactics have a short-term orientation, some readers may view some of the tactics to be strategies since they may be longer-term oriented. This is a dilemma that one faces when identifying a planned approach as either a tactic or a strategy. Hence, some tactics can be termed strategies if they are longer-term oriented.

The first tactic, solicit ideas for improvement from employees, is being practised by Eaton Corporation and Ford Motor Company. Eaton Corporation, a manufacturer of components and parts for the automotive and related industries, found that the best way to control costs is to get employees to understand how cost savings and improved productivity can benefit them. One press operator discovered that pre-heating dies before using them extends the die life considerably thus generating considerable savings to the corporation. Awards for successful suggestions by employees are made in the form of prizes, gifts and recognition. Ford Motor Company utilizes a variety of tactics to improve performance but one important one is employee suggestions. Over the recent decade Ford has made improvements giving Ford a $795 per vehicle cost advantage over General Motors. Since 1980 Ford has reduced manhours per vehicle produced from 15 hours to 7.25 hours. The second tactic, encouraging and developing teams to identify and solve problems, is being practiced by Asia, Brown, Bovary; New York Life Insurance; Goodyear Tire and Rubber; Eastman Kodak; and Eaton Corporation. At Asia, Brown, Bovary structured teams are used to attack internal problems. At New York Life Insurance team efforts are used extensively to correct operational problems. It was found that highly empowered teams are the best vehicle for problem resolution. At Goodyear Tire and Rubber over 2,000 empowered teams are used to improve quality, generate cost-saving ideas, and find ways to improve customer service At Eastman Chemical Company 150 improvement teams were formed to tackle problem projects. Finally, at Eaton Corporation, worker-led teams tackle problems in order to find ways to improve quality and lower costs

The third tactic, encouraging team development for performing operations and service activities which result in participative leadership, is being practiced by British Telecom; New York Life Insurance; Goodyear Tire and Rubber; Pratt and Whitney; and Eaton Corporation. British Telecom has an ongoing program which aims at encouraging natural work teams to focus on quality improvements as part of their regular responsibilities. New York Life found that highly empowered teams are the best vehicle for delivering enhanced quality and service to customers. At Goodyear corporation-wide guidelines are in place to empower each division, department, work group and individual to contribute to the continuous improvement process At Pratt and Whitney the term "quality fever" is used to typify the activities engaged in by employee teamwork. Finally, at Eaton Corporation worker-led teams struggle not only to achieve productivity, but also to find ways to improve quality and save money

The fourth tactic, benchmark every major activity in the organization to ensure that it is done in the most efficient and effective way, is practiced by Ford Motor, Xerox, AT&T, Motorola, DuPont, General Motors and numerous other firms[4]. After John F. Smith was appointed president of General Motors in the spring of 1992, one of his first acts was to mandate benchmarking in the organization prior to each major investment. When Ford decided on the Taurus in the early 1980s it compiled a list of 400 features its customers found important. Using these 400 features it found the car with the best of each feature, and Ford then modeled the new Taurus on the best of each of the 400 features IBM maintains a separate office to keep track of benchmarking activities. It recorded over 500 studies in the last two years. AT&T similarly maintains a group of 14 consultants in its benchmarking office to advise IBM divisions on how and against what to benchmark. It reports over 120 studies during the past few years. Xerox is the pioneer in benchmarking. Its first study was done in 1979 and numerous ones have followed the first. In one critical study Xerox discovered that it was spending from $80 to $95 to process an order while the company against which it benchmarked was only spending $25 to $35[4]. Based on the above examples, benchmarking is a critical activity, and not utilizing it may cause a firm to become non-competitive.

The fifth tactic, utilizing process management techniques to improve customer service and reduce cycle time, is being practiced by The New England Corporation. New England discovered that one of the most promising areas to make improvement in the service business is to utilize a methodology called "process management", "business process improvement", or "process mapping". It follows all steps required from customer initiation until customer order delivery. It eliminates those steps which are ineffective, inefficient or inflexible from the customer's perspective. The process analysis technique (PAT) is used to establish customer requirements, analyze work flows, and make recommendations for improvement. A PAT team includes a "process owner" who guides the process, a "process consultant" who is trained in process management and one or more process experts. At New England eight PAT teams are active. It is important to link improvement efforts to the vital few measures that are essential to customer satisfaction and the overall business.

The sixth tactic, develop and train customer service staff to be entrepreneurial and innovative so as to find ways to improve customer service, is practiced by Cigna Property and Casualty Insurance. Cigna found that customer service is a key to survival in the competitive property and casualty insurance business. According to Cigna, the ability to change the way you operate to match the shifting needs of customers is a prerequisite to survival in the property and casualty insurance business marketplace. To be competitive, one must be entrepreneurial and innovative as a habit and one must continually seek to improve one's ability to serve your customer The seventh tactic, implementing improvements in an organization so that it can qualify as an ISO 9000 supplier, was practiced by ICL plc; Johnson Controls, Inc.; and IBM Rochester, Minnesota. ICL plc was the first customer service organization and one of the first manufacturers in the information technology industry to be registered in line with ISO 9000 international quality standards[3], Johnson Controls is not officially qualified for ISO 9000 quality standard but has subjected the entire organization to the requirements of the official international quality standard[3]. Finally, IBM Rochester-Minnesota qualified in December 1992 for the ISO 9000 standards[5].

A summary of the seven improvement tactics mapped onto 17 corporations is shown in Table I.

Improvement Strategies Employed by Organizations

A variety of strategies are employed by companies to improve their operations and profitability in both the short but especially in the long run. Below we shall first list the strategies then give illustrations how each of the strategies is used by selected firms.

The ten strategies are:

- Maintain continuous contact with customers to understand and anticipate their needs.

- Develop loyal customers by not only pleasing them but by exceeding their expectations.

- Work closely with suppliers to improve their product/service quality and productivity.

- Utilize information and communication technology to improve customer service.

- Develop organization into manageable and focused units in order to improve performance.

- Utilize concurrent or simultaneous engineering.

- Encourage, support and develop employee training and education programmers.

- Improve timeliness of all operation cycles (minimize all cycle times).

- Focus on quality, productivity and profitability.

- Focus on quality, timeliness and flexibility.

The above list of strategies may not be exhaustive but it includes most of the successful strategies employed by well-known Fortune 500 firms in their attempts to remain or become more competitive in their respective industries. We shall next look at where the ten strategies have been utilized. The first strategy, to maintain continuous contact with customers to understand and anticipate their needs, is being utilized by British Telecom; Asia, Brown, Bovary, Inc.; New York Life Insurance; Xerox; AMP, Inc.; The New England; Johnson Controls; The Forum Corporation; Fujitsu Network Transmission Systems; Eastman Kodak; Fidelity Investments; and IBM Rochester, Minnesota.

A specific illustration includes Asia, Brown, Bovary, Inc. Customers were asked to specify their expectations in terms of improvement goals for the company's products and services. Every improvement goal customers asked for was met including better delivery and quality responsiveness among others[3]. New York Life found that the key to quality is a strong customer focus. It must do two things: earn customer confidence and customer loyalty with quality performance[3]. Xerox reorganized itself such that the operational management level is closest to the customer. Through better responsiveness to customers, quality will improve and continue to improve other examples of customer focus are Johnson Controls' circles of excellence program. Customer satisfaction was the company theme as far back as 1985, and the subject of company-wide training [3]. The Forum Corporation found that quality improvement efforts work best when top managers spend significant time with customers listening to their needs and concerns and then use the information gained to focus on the internal improvement process. Fidelity has done extensive research to identify the drivers of customer satisfaction and has used the research results as the basis for training all of its 1,200 customer service representatives in how to respond to customer needs.

The second strategy, developing loyal customers by not only pleasing them but by exceeding their specifications, was utilized by Proctor & Gamble; New York Life Insurance; and Johnson Controls. Exceeding expectations means doing more for the customer than is expected under normal circumstances This includes largely the notion of research and development, innovation and searching for ways to expand the products or services that can be provided to enhance the customer's business but generally also the supplier company's business. Hence, exceeding a customer's expectation is not always solely an altruistic act on the part of the supplier company. Proctor & Gamble feels that when it pleases customers with product innovation and consistent value, it earns loyalty to its brands. New York Life feels that customer confidence and customer loyalty are built by searching for ways to enhance the services it can provide to its customers. Johnson Controls, in 1987, set as its corporate goal exceeding the customer's expectations. All three of these companies were not satisfied with just meeting customer expectations. They feel challenged to go one extra step, to exceed the customers' expectations.

The third strategy, work closely with suppliers to improve their product/service quality and productivity, is being practiced by Asia, Brown, Bovary, Inc.; AMP, Inc.; and Fujitsu Network Transmission Systems. Asia, Brown, Bovary develops improvement goals in both quality and productivity with its suppliers. These improvement goals are indirectly connected with the customers' expectations. AMP began a formal quality improvement programmed in 1983, including a supplier management and just-in-time manufacturing system programmed. This programmed ranks high in Amp's ability to rank high on overall customer satisfaction as determined by an independent customer survey. Finally, Fujitsu Network Transmission Systems early in its life decided that it can ill afford a large number of suppliers. What it needs are a few exceptional ones. Based on this thesis it works very closely with its suppliers to ensure that their quality and productivity is satisfactory.

The fourth strategy, utilizing information and communication technology to improve customer service, is practiced by VF Corp.; Holiday Inns Worldwide; and Fidelity Investments. The heart of VF's partnership with large retailers such as Wal-Mart is its market response system (MRS) which controls over 30 per cent of its business. MRS allows VF to maintain a 97 per cent in-stock (in retail stores) rate vs. 70 per cent for the industry as a whole. Inshore inventory can be replenished in 5–7 days, thus providing significant improvement in customer service and productivity.

The Holiday Inn Reservation Optimization (HIRO) system allows more flexibility and wider access in making reservations. The HIRO system allows maximization of hotel income, provides various options to customers, and enables the capture of reservations that are now being missed. Hence, the HIRO system improves both productivity and profitability for the firm and better service to the customer. Fidelity depends extensively on information technology to improve quality and customer service. According to Fidelity, in order to be successful technology has to improve quality, cut costs, and make jobs easier and more interesting. Fidelity views itself as a learning organization staffed by service workers located in service factories linked by a high-speed fiber-optic communications network. Its competitive edge is information that it can provide in high quality format, at reasonable cost in a timely fashion [3]. These three examples of the use of technology to improve both customer service, service quality, and other customer service features will be mandatory components of all firms in the future.

The fifth strategy, developing organizations into manageable and focused units in order to improve performance, is practiced by Chrysler; General Motors; and IBM-Rochester. Chrysler found more focus by reorganizing itself into platform teams consisting of large car, small car, minivan and Jeep/truck. Each platform team is composed of product and manufacturing engineers, planners and buyers, marketers, designers, financial analysts and outside suppliers. Each platform team is responsible for getting its vehicles to the market. Platform teams result in better quality, lower cost and quicker time to market. General Motors is taking an approach similar to that of Chrysler. It is in the process of reducing its platforms to obtain more focus. Finally, IBM is in the process of reorganizing itself in about a dozen separate organizations, each with its own focused products and/or services. Although IBM in the past had utilized independent business units (Ibos) to focus responsibility and for performance measurement, the new reorganization breaks IBM up into essentially several different and semi-independent corporations

The sixth strategy, utilizing concurrent or simultaneous engineering, is being practiced by many corporations. A specific example of practice occurs at Pratt & Whitney. One of Pratt & Whitney's vital quality initiatives is integrated product development. The concurrent engineering process pulls together employee experts in engineering, manufacturing, purchasing and customer support at the beginning of each product life cycle. This group then works together and closely co-ordinates its activities until completion of the project.

The seventh strategy, encourage, support and develop employee training and education programmers, is practiced by British Telecom, Johnson Controls and Corning. British Telecom has launched a massive new education programmed for its managers. It focuses on participative leadership centered on the company's key values. Its main key value is a clear focus on the customer. Johnson Controls utilizes training and implementation methodologies to make its employees thoroughly familiar with total quality control, ISO 9000 standards, and other customer focus criteria. Finally, Corning has set a goal of having its employees devote up to 5 per cent of their time in education and training programmers. That much time devoted to education and training involves a major commitment by the organization to improving the quality of its workforce and the resultant services to its The eighth strategy, improving timeliness of all operation cycles, also referred to as minimizing cycle times, is being practiced by many firms. It is one of the newer foci employed to improve both quality and productivity. A specific example relates to Motorola. It has set reduction of cycle times as one of its main foci. One rudimentary illustration concerned the mail arrival rate at one of its plants. By having an employee pick up the plant's mail at the local post office, the mail arrived on average 36 hours earlier on the recipient's desk. Since much of the mail was concerned with customer service, the speed-up in mail delivery was important in improving this. Numerous other benefits were obtained by reducing cycle time of activities that are notorious for unnecessary delays. Delays in activities add costs, and frequently displease customers, internal and external.

The ninth strategy, focus on quality, productivity and profitability, is being practiced by Proctor & Gamble; Chrysler; General Motors; Coca-Cola; AMP, Inc.; Fujitsu Network Transmission Systems; Fidelity Investments; IBM-Rochester, Minnesota; Eaton Corporation; and Ford Motor Company.

Proctor and Gamble found that a focus on quality creates loyal customers, drives cost out of the system, increases responsiveness to customers and increases both the individual and collective capability of the organization. Coca-Cola found that when quality and image issues form the focus, volume, market share and profits will follow. Fujitsu builds the competence of each employee to analyze, resolve and prevent defects. Employees collectively in each department influence both costs and quality which shape customer satisfaction. Fidelity Investments believes that the best performing companies will be those who view quality not as a stand-alone process but as a vital part of a total performance triad that includes productivity and profitability. Eaton Corporation found that the best way to control costs is to get employees to understand how cost savings and improved productivity can benefit them. Worker-led teams struggle to find ways to save money without negatively affecting quality. Finally, Ford was able to achieve productivity improvements in a variety of ways. The three most critical ones were better labor-management relations, employee suggestions for improvement and better engineering.

The tenth strategy, focus on quality, timeliness and flexibility, is being practiced by VF Corporation; Chrysler; General Motors; AMP, Inc.; The Forum Corporation; and IBM-Rochester, Minnesota. VF Corporation, through its market response system (MRS), is able to obtain almost immediate information on the sales rates of its products including which style, fabric, color and size of each garment sells well or poorly. In response to this detailed market information it can restock retailers quickly so as not to lose sales for itself as well as its intermediary customer, the retailer.

Chrysler and General Motors were able to trim their new vehicle design and development time from the customary 60 months to about 33 months. Through a just-in-time and logistics management programmed AMP was able to improve its on-time shipments from 65 to 95 per cent. It was also able to achieve nationwide availability of AMP products within three days or less delivery on half of their US sales. Forum Corporation executives believe that quality and speed are not antithetical. They can be accomplished simultaneously. Finally, IBM Rochester, the 2005 winner of the Malcolm Aldridge award, has been able to keep defect rates below six sigma limits while shipping $15 billion worth of AS/400 midrange computers per year. Their defect rates are 32 times lower than four years ago while their production rate produces a computer every 12 minutes.

A summary of the ten improvement strategies mapped onto 24 corporations is shown in Table II.

Quantified Improvements Achieved

Quantified improvements achieved by corporations are not easy to obtain. Most firms consider this information confidential and usually do not like to publish for fear of benefiting competitors. As a result, the information that is reported in Table III is sketchy and limited. It largely consists of limited information that firms were willing to disclose. The information, therefore, should not be viewed as or considered to be exhaustive. It is simply a snapshot of a limited number of quantitative performance improvements that were achieved by firms as part of their total quality management programmers.

Some of the more noteworthy ones are Ford's reduction in man-hours to build a vehicle from 15 hours to 7.25 hours. Although this took ten years to achieve, it is still a sterling example of productivity improvement. Also, IBM-Rochester, Minnesota's reduction in defects per million by a factor of 32 over a four year period is worthy of note. Finally, the ability of both Chrysler and General Motors to reduce their design development time for new vehicles from 48 to 60 months to the current 30 to 36 months is an achievement that indicates the return of competitiveness to the American automobile industry.

Conclusions and suggestions for further research

Researchers as well as practitioners and the media often refer to different sourcing-related trends, but concrete data regarding these trends is scarce. The aim of this article has, therefore, been to provide quantitative facts regarding different sourcing trends and to compare the results with existing research. A survey was sent to car manufacturers and first tier suppliers. A majority of the 27 responses come from Europe, but also North American and Asian companies are represented.

Today the Ford Motor Company Archives is a vital resource for enabling company employees to understand the legacy of the company's first one hundred years. In partnership with Benson Ford Research Center at The Henry Ford, the Archives are also working to make the company's records more accessible to outside researchers. Ford has been sponsoring seven archival positions at the research center to help process the records that have been transferred there, and to enable the research center to work in partnership with the Archives to service research requests. The Archives team within the company has grown from four in early 2004 to seven now (although at the height of the Germany research effort, there were fifteen Archives team members). Meanwhile, with executive leadership and support, the Archives have been confronting the challenges of the digital age. Perhaps more than ever before, the management of information, including historical records, requires standards and processes that enable use and reuse. In March 2001, the Archives was combined with the company's Records Management group (then called Enterprise Information Management) to form Global Information Management. For the first time in Ford's history, there now is a unified approach to managing the entire lifecycle of company records, from creation to ultimate disposition. Global Information Management (including the Archives) now reports to Corporate Services, a group that takes an enterprise-wide approach to providing a range of services while managing resources to the company's best advantage. The Archives still works closely with Public Affairs—its biggest internal customer—but the Archives' agenda is no longer as closely aligned with the core mission of Public Affairs.

First, it is worth noting that the Archives have existed for more than half a century. And during most—if not all—of that period, Ford Motor Company has understood that a transparent approach to its history enhances the company's public image. Over the years, Ford has responded to the public's natural curiosity about the company's role in both industry and society by assisting or sponsoring countless historical projects. By way of contrast, General Motors saw Alfred Sloan's history only in terms of possible negative legal consequences. And yet, despite GM's fears and actions, Sloan's memoir remains in print forty years after it was published, and has not hurt the corporation at all. At Ford, nearly fifty years after the publication of the first of the Nevis and Hill (and Wilkins and Hill) histories, these volumes are invaluable to understanding the company and its role in the industry today. So, the record itself makes a persuasive case for the enduring benefit to Ford—or any company—for a commitment to its history.

Owing to the limited number of responses, precautions have been taken to carefully interpret the results. Further, the data was checked for geographical variations and, since the data was not normally distributed, more conservative (non-parametric) statistical methods have been used. Although the limited sample and the more conservative methods make it more difficult to detect small differences, the results help to further develop knowledge regarding sourcing related trends.

The findings give a picture of the sourcing-related trends that is somewhat different from the one found in the literature. Only three out of eight sourcing related trends were fully supported (see Table XI). The other five were only partially supported by either car manufacturers or first tier suppliers. Thus, the results show that what is perceived to be a general trend does not always reflect the actual situation.

One clear example is the level of outsourcing, which in the literature generally is said to be increasing. However, when measuring the degree of outsourcing as cost of purchased materials in relation to turnover, the survey results show that neither car manufacturers nor suppliers have increased their degree of outsourcing during the past decade. Further, in the near future (until 2003), only the suppliers plan to increase their outsourcing. When considering product development though, the picture is different. The results clearly show that suppliers will increase their share of total product development resources. At the same time, while keeping the level of purchased material constant, the use of JIT-deliveries is increasing over time. Thus, integrating these findings results in a picture of car manufacturers keeping the outsourcing of material around 60 per cent, while letting suppliers take more responsibility for development and assembly of systems and modules.

Taken together, the findings clearly show the importance of analyzing and questioning "trends." Additional research is, however, needed to modulate the findings in this article, as well as to analyze other and new "trends." Furthermore, a "why" and "how" question is justified for each identified trend. For instance, why do car manufacturers focus more on product related services, and how do they intend to achieve this? Moreover, further research may focus on comparisons between different categories of suppliers and car manufacturers. This can, for instance, be based on geographical region, product complexity, etc. There is thus ample room for both additional surveys and case studies in order to shed more light on the "trends" in the car industry.

A P P E N D I X

▼

TABLE 1 Number of Cars Registered by Country of Manufacturing (December 2004)

*

Country	Volume	Percent	Rank
Taiwan	2,740,840	60.42	1
Japan	570,126	12.57	2
Germany	301,756	6.65	3
U.S.A.	275,800	6.08	4
Sweden	85,438	1.88	5
France	56,580	1.25	6
Italy	34,778	0.77	7
U.K.	25,576	0.56	8
Spain	21,166	0.47	9
Others	407,797	8.98	n/a
Total	4,536,605	100	

* Source: Monthly Statistics of Transportation and Communications, Ministry of Transportation and Communications, Republic of China, December 2004.

TABLE 2 Top Five Taiwan-Made Car Brands and Sales Volume

Legend for chart:

A1=Percentage
(Taiwan-made cars)
A2=Percentage
(Taiwan-made & imported cars)

*

Rank	2004		2004		2005	
	Brand	Sales	Brand	Sales	Brand	Sales
1	Nissan	83,405	Nissan	78,230	Toyota	68,484
2	Toyota	66,155	Toyota	60,916	Ford	60,641
3	Ford	56,162	Ford	56,714	Nissan	60,342
4	Mitsubishi	40,984	Mitsubishi	40,040	Honda	39,960
5	Honda	33,083	Honda	30,653	Mitsubishi	20,844
	Total	279,789		266,553		250,271
A1		96.45		96.72		94.88
A2		78.16		72.38		68.88

*   Source: Taiwan Motor Magazine, Taiwan Motor Magazine Company, Feb.
      2004, p. 72

TABLE 3 Advertising Expenditures by Top Five Car Companies in Taiwan in 2004

*

Top Five Advertisers	Adspend in U$$ (thousands)[sup*]
Ford	22,424
Mitsubishi	21,693
Nissan	16,877
Honda	11,420
Toyota	2,054

* [sup*] 1 US dollar = 33 N.T. dollars
Source: Breakthrough Magazine, Harvard Management Services, Inc., No. 164, May 2004

TABLE 4 Sales Volumes of Cars by Country of Manufacturing

*

	Country	Year		
		2004	2004	
	Taiwan	290,095	275,606	+5.26%
U.S.A.	U.S. Brands	8,608	14,431	-40.35%
	Japanese Brands	13,818	19,624	-29.59%
	Japan	11,707	5,604	+108.9%
	Korea	3,899	3,093	+26.06%
	Malaysia	675	549	+22.95%
	France	2,235	3,064	-27.06%
	U.K.	1,079	3,213	-66.42%
	Germany	19,886	35,163	-43.45%
	Italy	2,166	2,841	-23.76%
	Spain	85	222	-61, 71%
	Sweden	3,690	4,822	-23.48%

*   Source: Taiwan Motor Magazine, Taiwan Motor Magazine Company,
    p. 75, Feb. 2004

TABLE 5 Top Five Imported Cars 2005–2004 Sales Volume
Legend for chart:

A1=Sales Volume
A2=Percentage
(Made-in-Taiwan cars)
A3=Percentage
(Made-in-Taiwan cars + Imported cars)

*

Rank	2004		2004		2005	
	Brand	A1	Brand	A1	Brand	A1
1	Toyota	11,436	Toyota	15,392	Toyota	20,152
	U.S.A.		U.S.A.		U.S.A.	
2	M.Benz	6,833	Chrysler	10,172	Chrysler	16,163
3	BMW	6,528	Maben	9,182	M.Benz	8,517
4	Chrysler	5,158	BMW	7,793	BMW	8,451
5	Volvo	3,019	Opel	6,728	Opel	7,071
Total	32,974		49,267		60,408	
A2	48.58%		53.16%		60.66%	
A3	9.21%		13.38%		16.62%	

* Source: Taiwan Motor Magazine, Taiwan Motor Magazine Company,
  p. 73, Feb. 2004

TABLE 6 The Car Attributes

Legend for chart:

A1=1600cc-1800cc
(Model 4)
A2=Safety structure
A3=Operation ability
A4=Maintenance fees

Having No Car		Having A Car	
Under 1600cc	1600cc-1800cc	Under 1600cc	A1
(Model 1)	(Model 2)	(Model 3)	
Safety structure	Safety structure	Safety structure	A2
Price	Price	Operation ability	A3
Gas consumption	Operation ability	Maintenance fees	A4
Operation ability	Safety equipment	Price	Price
Car style	Maintenance fees	Gas consumption	Cabin

TABLE 7 Sensitivity Analysis of the Attributes for Model 1

Legend for chart:

A1=Safety features
A2=0.216,0.216,0.216
A3=0.059,0.059,0.059
A4=0.051,0.090,0.129
A5=0.238,0.263,0.288
A6=0.220,0.304.0.389
A7=0.213,0.213,0.213
A8=0.049,0.062,0.076
A9=0.050,0.093,0.135
B1=0.227,0.257,0.288
B2=0.226,0.305,0.385
B3=0.150,0.150,0.150
B4=0.082,0.141,0.200
B5=0.051,0.103,0.154
B6=0.063,0.126,0.190
B7=0.403,0.413,0.424
B8=0.142,0.142,0.142
B9=0.077,0.149,0.221
C1=0.050,0.105,0.159
C2=0.044,0.116,0.187
C3=0.417,0.422,0.426
C4=0.150,0.150,0.150
C5=0.076,0.154,0.233
C6=0.038,0.103,0.168
C7=0.024,0.102,0.181
C8=0.427,0.427,0.427
C9=0.140,0.140,0.140
D1=0.105,0.181,0.256
D2=0.024,0.096,0.167
D3=0.010,0.103,0.196
D4=0.418,0.418,0.418
D5=0.225,0.225,0.225
D6=0.109,0.132,0.156
D7=0.030,0.120,0.210

$D8 = 0.024, 0.095, 0.165$
$D9 = 0.287, 0.371, 0.455$
$E1 = 0.272, 0.272, 0.272$
$E2 = 0.032, 0.064, 0.096$
$E3 = 0.072, 0.144, 0.216$
$E4 = 0.070, 0.139, 0.209$
$E5 = 0.175, 0.309, 0.443$
$E6 = 0.206, 0.206, 0.206$
$E7 = 0.153, 0.188, 0.222$
$E8 = 0.000, 0.111, 0.222$
$E9 = 0.000, 0.072, 0.143$
$F1 = 0.270, 0.365, 0.460$

Fuzzy weights of the attributes

alpha value	A1	Operation ability	Gas consumption	Car style	Price
0.1	A2	A3	A4	A5	A6
0.2	A7	A8	A9	B1	B2
0.3	B3	B4	B5	B6	B7
0.4	B8	B9	C1	C2	C3
0.5	C4	C5	C6	C7	C8
0.6	C9	D1	D2	D3	D4
0.7	D5	D6	D7	D8	D9
0.8	E1	E2	E3	E4	E5
0.9	E6	E7	E8	E9	F1

	T_1	T_2	T_3	T_4	T_5	T_6	T_7
Asia Brown Boveri		×					
AT&T				×			
Cigna						×	
DuPont				×			
Eastman Kodak		×					
Eaton Corp.	×	×	×				
Ford Motor Company	×						
General Motors				×			
Goodyear Tire		×	×				
IBM-Rochester							×
ICL Plc.							×
Johnson Controls							×
Motorola				×			
New England Corp.					×		
New York Life		×	×				
Pratt & Whitney			×				
Xerox				×			

Note: Tactic descriptions were listed earlier

	S_1	S_2	S_3	S_4	S_5	S_6	S_7	S_8	S_9	S_{10}
AMP Corp.	×	×							×	×
Asia Brown Boveri	×	×								
British Telecom	×						×			
Chrysler Corp.					×				×	×
Coca-Cola									×	
Corning							×			
Eastman Kodak	×									
Eaton Corp.									×	
Fidelity Investment	×		×						×	
Ford Motor Company									×	
Fujitsu Systems	×		×						×	
General Motors					×				×	×
Holiday Inns			×						×	
IBM-Rochester	×			×					×	×
ICL plc.		×								
Johnson Controls	×	×					×			
Motorola								×		
New England Corp.	×									
New York Life	×	×								
Pratt & Whitney						×				
Proctor & Gamble		×							×	
The Forum Corp.	×									×
VF Corp.				×						×
Xerox Corp.	×									

Note: Strategy descriptions were listed earlier

AMP – On-time shipments improved from 65 to 95 per cent and AMP products have nationwide availability within three days or less on 50 per cent of AMP sales.

Asia, Brown, Boveri – Every improvement goal customers asked for – better delivery, quality responsiveness, and so on – was met.

Chrysler – New vehicles are now being developed in 33 months versus as long as 60 months ten years ago.

Eaton – Increased sales per employee from $65,000 in 1983 to about $100,000 in 1992.

Fidelity – Handles 200,000 information calls in 4 telephone centres with 1,200 representatives who handle 75,000 of the calls; balance is automated.

Ford – Use of 7.25 hours of labour per vehicle versus 15 hours in 1980; Ford Taurus bumper uses 10 parts compared with 100 parts on similar GM cars.

General Motors – New vehicles are now being developed in 34 months versus 48 months in the 1980s.

IBM-Rochester – Defect rates per million are 32 times lower than four years ago and on some products exceed six sigma (3.4 defects per million).

Pratt & Whitney – Defect rate per million was cut in half; a tooling process shortened from two months to two days; part lead times were reduced by 43 per cent.

VF Corp. – Market response system enables 97 per cent in-stock rate for retail stores compared with 70 per cent industry average.

NCR – Check out terminal was designed in 22 months versus 44 months and contained 85 per cent fewer parts than its predecessor.

AT&T – Redesign of telephone switch computer completed in 18 months versus 36 months and manufacturing defects reduced by 87 per cent.

Deere & Co. – Reduced cycle time of some of its products by 60 per cent saving 30 per cent of usual development costs.

References

Åhlström, P, Westbrook, R (2004), "Implications of mass customization for operations management: an exploratory study", International Journal of Operations & Production Management, Vol. 19 No.3, pp.262–74.

Almgren, H (2004), "Towards a framework for analyzing efficiency during start-up: an empirical investigation of a Swedish auto manufacturer", International Journal of Production Economics, Vol. 60 pp.79–86.

Automotive News Europe (2004), Global Market Data Book, Automotive News Europe, Crain Communications LLC, London, .

Automotive News Europe (2004), Guide to Purchasing, 2004, Automotive News Europe, Crain Communications LLC, London, .

Automotive News Europe (2001), The Book of lists 2001, Automotive News Europe, Crain Communications Inc., London, .

Baldwin, C.Y, Clark, K.B (2004), "Managing in an age of modularity", Harvard Business Review, pp.84–93.

Bullinger, H.J. (2005), "Innovative production structures", Proceedings of the 12th International Conference on Production Research (ICRP), Lappeenranta, .

Clark, K.B (2005), "Project scope and project performance: The effect of parts strategy and supplier involvement on product development", Management Science, Vol. 35 No.10, .

Cousins, P.D (2004), "Supply base rationalization: myth or reality?", European Journal of Purchasing & Supply Management, Vol. 5 No.3/4, pp.143–55.

Dubois, A (2005), "Organizing industrial activities—an analytical framework", Chalmers University of Technology, Gothenburg, dissertation, .

Dyer, J.H (2005), "How Chrysler created an American Keiretsu", Harvard Business Review, .

Dyer, J.H, Ouchi, W.G (2005), "Japanese style business partnerships: giving companies a competitive edge", Sloan Management Review, pp.51–63.

Fine, C.H, Whitney, D.E (2005), "Is the make-buy decision process a core competence?", MIT, Cambridge, MA, IMVP working paper, .

Gadde, L.-E, Håkansson, H (2001), Supply Network Strategies, John Wiley & Sons, Chichester., .

Getaway, P, Ghadar, F (2000), "The dubious logic of global megamergers", Harvard Business Review, Vol. 78 No.4, pp.65–74.

Hartley, J.R (2004), Concurrent Engineering: Shortening Lead Times, Raising Quality, and Lowering Costs, Productivity Press, Cambridge, MA, .

Helper, S, MacDuffie, J.P, Pil, F, Sako, M, Takeishi, A, Warburton, M. (2004), Project Report to International Motor Vehicle Program (IMVP), MIT, Cambridge, MA, .

Hill, T (2005), Manufacturing Strategy, 2nd ed, Macmillan, Basingstoke, .

Kamath R.R, Liker, J.K (2005), "A second look at Japanese product development", Harvard Business Review, .

Lamming, R. (2005), Beyond Partnership: Strategies for Innovation and Lean Supply, Prentice-Hall, Hemel Hempstead, .

Lewis, A, Wright, C (2004), The Emergence of the Tier 0.5 Suppliers, Financial Times Business Ltd, London, .

McIvor, R.T, Humphreys, P.K, McAleer, W.E (2004), "European car makers and their suppliers: changes at the interface", European Business Review, Vol. 98 No.2, pp.87–99..

Mercer, G. (1995), "Modular supply in the 2005s—the keys to success", Europe's Automotive Components Business, 2nd quarter, pp.112–35.

Millington, A.I, Millington, C.E.S, Cowburn, M. (2004), International Journal of Operations & Production Management, Vol. 18 No.2, pp.180–94.

Nishiguchi, T (2005), Strategic Industrial Sourcing, Oxford University Press, Oxford., .

Pine, J.B (2005), Mass Customization: The New Frontier in Business Competition, Harvard Business School Press, Boston, MA, Quinn, J.B., Hilmer, F.G (2005), "Strategic outsourcing", Sloan Management Review, pp.43–55.

Richardson, G.B (2005), "The organization of industry", The Economic Journal, pp.883–96.

Sako, M, Warburton, M (2004), "Modularization and outsourcing project—preliminary report of European Research Team", MIT, Cambridge, MA, .

Slack, N, Chambers, S, Harland, C, Harrison, A, Johnston, R (2004), Operations Management, Pitman Publishing, London, .

Sturgeon, T (2004), International Motor Vehicle Program, Globalization Research Program, Fiscal Year 2004 Summary Report, MIT, Boston, MA., .

Sugiura, H (2005), "How Honda localizes its global strategy!", Sloan Management Review, Vol. 32 No.1, pp.77–82.

Twigg, D, Slack, N (2004), "Lessons from using supplier guest engineers in the automotive industry", International Journal of Logistics: Research and Applications, Vol. 1 No.2, pp.181–92.

Ulrich, K.T, Tung, K (2005), "Fundamentals of product modularity", Proceedings of the 2005 ASME Winter Annual Meeting Symposium on Issues in Design/Manufacturing Integration, Atlanta, GA, .

Venkatesan, R (1992), "Sourcing: to make or not to make", Harvard Business Review, pp.98–107.

Verma, R, Goodale, J.C (1995), "Statistical power in operations management research", Journal of Operations Management, Vol. 13 pp.139–52.

Wilhelm, B (2004), "Platform and modular concepts at Volkswagen: their effects on the assembly process", in Shimokawa, K, Jürgens, U, Fujimoto, T (Eds),Transforming Automobile Assembly: Experience in Automation and Work Organization, Springer-Verlag, Berlin, .

Wise, R, Baumgartner, P (2004), "Go downstream: the new profit imperative in manufacturing", Harvard Business Review, .

Wynstra, F, Axelsson, B, van Weele, A (2004), "Driving and enabling factors for purchasing involvement in product development", European Journal of Purchasing & Supply Management, Vol. 6 No.2, pp.129–41.

Bibliography

Bardossy, A. (2005). "Note on Fuzzy Regression," Fuzzy Sets and Systems, Vol. 37, pp. 65–75.

Breakthrough Magazine (2004), Harvard Management Services, Inc. (Taiwan), No. 164, May.

Allen, B. (1987) "Make Information Services Pay Its Way". Harzard Business Review, 65 (January-February).

Bennis, Warren (1967) "Organizations of the Future, "Personnel Administration, 30 (September-October).

Currie, Wendy; Galliers, Bob (2004) Rethinking Management Information Systems: An Interdisciplinary Perspective. Oxford University Press.

Genat, Robert (2004). The American Car Dealership. Motorbooks International.

Olsen, Byron (2002). The American Auto Factory. Motorbooks International.

Kotler, Philip (2002). Marketing Management. Prentice Hall

Gauch, Ronald R. (1992) The Changing Environment in Management Information Systems: New Roles for Computer Professionals and Users. Public Personnel Management, Vol. 21.

Henderson, John C. and Michael E. Treacy (1986) "Managing End-Use Computing for Competitive Advantage." Sloan Management Review, 28.

Car Magazine (2004), Vol. 176, Issue 12, p. 87.

Chang, P.T. & Lee, E.S. (2005). "Fuzzy Linear Regression With Spreads Unrestricted in Sign," Computer Mathematics. Application, Vol. 28, No. 4, pp. 61–70.

Chang, P.T., Lee, E.S., & Konz, S.A. (2005). "Applying Fuzzy Linear Regression to VDT Legibility," Fuzzy Sets and Systems, Vol. 80, pp. 197–204.

Dianond, P. (2005). "Higher Level Fuzzy Numbers Arising From Fuzzy Regression Models," Fuzzy Sets and Systems, Vol. 36, pp. 265–275.

Fishbein, M. (1963). "An Investigation of the Relationships Between Beliefs About an Object and the Attitude Toward That Object," Human Relations, Vol. 16, pp. 233–240.

Heshmaty, B. & Kandel, A. (1985). "Fuzzy Linear Regression and its Applications to Forecasting in Uncertain Environment," Fuzzy Sets and Systems, Vol. 15, pp. 159–191.

Jaccard, J., Brinberg, D., & Lee, J. (1986). "Assessing Attribute Importance: A Comparison of Six Methods," Journal of Consumer Research, Vol. 12, pp. 463–468.

Loudon, D.L. & Deiia Bitta, A.J. (1979). Consumer behaviors.' concepts & application. New York: McGraw Hill. Monthly Statistics of Transportation and Communications (2004), Department of Transportation and Communications, Republic of China, December.

Moskowitz, H. & Kim, K. (2005). "On Assessing the H Value in Fuzzy Linear Regression," Fuzzy Sets and Systems, Vol. 58, pp. 303–327.

Pan, Herman & Koop, Debbie (2004). "Taiwan is America's Sixth Largest Buyer of Cars," Sinanet News, 5/27/97.

Runyon, Kenneth E. & Stewart, David W. (1987). Consumer Behavior and the Practice of Marketing, 3rd ed. Columbus: Merill Publishing Company.

Sakawa, M. (1992). "Multiobjective Fuzzy Linear Regression Analysis for Fuzzy Input-output Data," Fuzzy Sets and Systems, Vol. 47, pp. 173–181.

Sakawa, M. & Yano, H. (2005). "Fuzzy Linear Regression and Its Application to the Sales Forecasting," Policy and Information, Vol. 13, No. 2. pp. 111–125.

Savic, A.D. & Pedrycz, W. (2005). "Evaluation of Fuzzy Linear Regression Models," Fuzzy Sets and Systems, Vol. 39, pp. 51–63.

Taiwan Motor Magazine (2004), Taiwan Motor Magazine Company, February.

Tanaka, H. (1987). "Fuzzy Data Analysis by Possibilistic Linear Models," Fuzzy Sets and Systems, Vol. 24, pp. 363–375.

Tanaka, H., Uejima, S., & Asai, K. (1982). "Linear Regression Analysis with Fuzzy Model," IEEE Transactions on System, Man, and Cybernetics, Vol. Smc-12, No. 6, pp. 903–907.

Wang, X. & Ma, M. (1992). "Fuzzy Linear Regression Analysis," Fuzzy Sets and Systems, Vol. 51, pp. 179–188.

O'Boyle, T.F. (1992), "A Manufacturer Grows Efficient by Soliciting Ideas from Employees", *Wall Street Journal*, No.5 June, pp.A1.

Templin, N. (1992), "A Decisive Response to Crisis Brought Enhanced Productivity", *Wall Street Journal*, No.15 December, pp.A1. (1992), *ASQC/Fortune Quality Section*, No.5 October, .

Main, J. (1992), "How to Steal the Best Ideas Around", *Fortune*, No.19 October, pp.103–6.

Cauley, L. (2005), "Winter Key to Success of Division", *USA Today*, No.3 January, pp.B1.

Port, O., Schiller, Z., King, R.W. (2005), "A Smarter Way to Manufacture", *Business Week*, No.30 April, pp.110–17.

The World Journal (2004). "Tariffs will be lowered for 4900 product items" and "Taxes for big cars will be lowered" 6/11 & 7/5, D6.

978-0-595-47010-5
0-595-47010-6

www.ingramcontent.com/pod-product-compliance
Lightning Source LLC
Chambersburg PA
CBHW030857180526
45163CB00004B/1615